Poverty, Participation, and Democracy

A Global Perspective

For too long a conventional wisdom has held sway suggesting that poor people in poor countries are not supportive of democracy and that democracies will be sustained only after a certain average level of wealth has been achieved. Evidence from twenty-four diverse countries of Asia, Africa, and Latin America examined in this volume shows that poor people do not value democracy any less than their richer counterparts. Their faith in democracy is as high as that of other citizens, and they participate in democratic activities as much as their richer counterparts. Democracy is not likely to be unstable or unwelcome simply because poverty is widespread. Political attitudes and participation levels are unaffected by relative wealth. Education, rather than income or wealth, makes for more committed and engaged democratic citizens. Investments in education will make a critical difference for stabilizing and strengthening democracy.

Anirudh Krishna (PhD in government, Cornell University 2000; master's degree in economics, University of Delhi 1980) is Associate Professor of Public Policy and Political Science at Duke University. His books include *Active Social Capital: Tracing the Roots of Development and Democracy* (2002); *Community Experiences in Poverty Reduction* (2000); *Reasons for Success: Learning from Instructive Experiences in Rural Development* (1998); *Changing Policy and Practice from Below: Community Experiences in Poverty Reduction* (2000); and *Reasons for Hope: Instructive Experiences in Rural Development* (1997). His articles have appeared in *Comparative Politics, Comparative Political Studies, Development and Change, Journal of Asian Studies, Journal of Development Studies, Journal of Human Development, Journal of Politics, Public Administration and Development,* and *World Development.* He received the American Political Science Association's prize for best article in comparative democratization for an article published in *Comparative Political Studies* in May 2002. Another article, published in the *Journal of Development Studies,* won the Dudley Seers Memorial Prize in 2005.

10669056

Poverty, Participation, and Democracy

A Global Perspective

ANIRUDH KRISHNA
Duke University

CAMBRIDGE
UNIVERSITY PRESS

CAMBRIDGE UNIVERSITY PRESS
Cambridge, New York, Melbourne, Madrid, Cape Town, Singapore, São Paulo, Delhi

Cambridge University Press
32 Avenue of the Americas, New York, NY 10013-2473, USA

www.cambridge.org
Information on this title: www.cambridge.org/9780521729604

First published 2008

Printed in the United States of America

A catalog record for this publication is available from the British Library.

Library of Congress Cataloging in Publication Data

Poverty, participation, and democracy : a global perspective / Anirudh Krishna.
   p.   cm.
Includes bibliographical references and index.
ISBN 978-0-521-50445-4 (hardback) – ISBN 978-0-521-72960-4 (pbk.)
1. Poor – Research – Developing countries.   2. Poor – Political activity.
3. Poor – Attitudes.   4. Political participation.   5. Democracy.
I. Krishna, Anirudh.   II. Title.
HC79.P6P6857   2008
323′.042086942–dc22   2008001453

ISBN 978-0-521-50445-4 hardback
ISBN 978-0-521-72960-4 paperback

For Aditi and Abhay

Contents

Preface

The idea for this volume took root at a workshop on poverty and democracy organized at Duke University on February 17 and 18, 2006. Thanks are due to the sponsors of this workshop: the Center on Markets and Democratic Institutions (MADI); the Program for the Study of Democracy, Institutions and Political Economy (DIPE); and the Duke Center for International Development (DCID).

Contributors

John A. Booth is Regents Professor of Political Science at the University of North Texas. He is the author of *Costa Rica: Quest for Democracy* (1998) and *The End and the Beginning: The Nicaraguan Revolution* (1985), and the co-author of *Understanding Central America* (2006). He is co-editor of and contributor to *Political Participation in Latin America*; *The Politics of San Antonio*; *Community, Power, and Progress*; *Elections and Democracy in Central America*; and *Elections and Democracy in Central America Revisited*. He is the author or co-author of articles in *American Journal of Political Science, Journal of Politics, Political Research Quarterly, Latin American Research Review, Latin American Politics and Society, American Behavioral Scientist, Western Political Quarterly, Comparative Political Studies, Journal of Inter-American Studies and World Affairs, America Latina, Current History,* and other journals. He has lectured and consulted on Latin American politics for the Department of State, the United States Agency for International Development, public interest groups, and private corporations; was Fulbright Lecturer in International Relations in Costa Rica, 1979–1980; and served as an election observer in Nicaragua (1984, 1990, 1996, 2001) and Guatemala (1985). He received (with co-author Mitchell Seligson) the Hoover Institution Prize for the best article on Latin American politics published in 1984 and was the Latin American Studies Association's XVII International Congress program chair in 1991–1992.

Michael Bratton is professor in the Department of Political Science and African Studies Center at Michigan State University (MSU). In 2006 he was the recipient of a university-wide Distinguished Faculty Award. He is also a founder and the director of the Afrobarometer, a collaborative, international, survey research project that measures public opinion on democracy, markets, and civil society in eighteen African countries. Professor Bratton received a PhD from Brandeis University and joined the MSU faculty in 1977. He has held a postdoctoral fellowship from the Rockefeller Foundation, served as a program officer with the Ford Foundation, and been a visiting scholar at the University of Natal (South Africa), the University of Zimbabwe, and Uppsala University (Sweden). In 2006, he spent a semester at Oxford University. Bratton's main research and teaching interests are in comparative politics (democratization, social movements, and public opinion) and policy studies (development policy, development administration, and evaluation research). His current research focuses on public opinion in new democracies, particularly in sub-Saharan Africa, but also in broad comparative perspective. He is the author of sixty-five articles and book chapters, including contributions to *World Politics, British Journal of Political Science, Comparative Politics, Comparative Political Studies, Journal of Democracy*, and *World Development*. His latest books are *Democratic Experiments in Africa: Regime Transitions in Comparative Perspective*, with Nicolas van de Walle (1997) and *Public Opinion, Democracy and Market Reform in Africa*, with Robert Mattes and E. Gyimah-Boadi (2005).

Anirudh Krishna is Associate Professor of Public Policy and Political Science at Duke University. His research investigates how poor communities and individuals in developing countries cope with the structural and personal constraints that result in poverty and powerlessness. His books include *Active Social Capital: Tracing the Roots of Development and Democracy* (2002); *Reasons for Success: Learning from Instructive Experiences in Rural Development* (1998); *Changing Policy and Practice from Below: Community Experiences in Poverty Reduction* (2000); and *Reasons for Hope: Instructive Experiences in Rural Development* (1997). His articles have appeared in *Comparative*

Politics, Comparative Political Studies, Development and Change, Journal of Asian Studies, Journal of Development Studies, Journal of Human Development, Journal of Politics, Public Administration and Development, and *World Development.* He received the American Political Science Association's prize for best article in comparative democratization for his article published in *Comparative Political Studies* in May 2002. Another article, published in the *Journal of Development Studies,* won the Dudley Seers Memorial Prize in 2005.

Adam Przeworski is the Carroll and Milton Professor of Politics at New York University. Previously, he taught at the University of Chicago, where he was the Martin A. Ryerson Distinguished Service Professor, and held visiting appointments in India, Chile, France, Germany, Spain, and Switzerland. A member of the American Academy of Arts and Sciences since 1991, he was the recipient of the 1997 Lubbert Prize and the 2001 Woodrow Wilson Prize. He is the author or co-author of thirteen books and numerous articles, translated into seventeen languages. His recent publications include *States and Markets* (2003), *Democracy and the Rule of Law* (2003), and *Democracy and Development* (2000).

Mitchell A. Seligson is the Centennial Professor of Political Science at Vanderbilt University and is also a Fellow of the Center for the Americas at Vanderbilt. He founded and directs the Latin American Public Opinion Project (LAPOP), which has received generous support from the United States Agency for International Development (USAID) and the United Nations Development Programme (UNDP). LAPOP has conducted more than forty surveys of public opinion, mainly focused on democracy in many countries in Latin America but more recently including projects in Africa. He also served as director of the Center for Latin American Studies at the University of Pittsburgh. He has held grants and fellowships from the Rockefeller Foundation, the Ford Foundation, the National Science Foundation, The Howard Heinz Foundation, Fulbright, USAID, and others, and he has published more than eighty articles and more than a dozen books and monographs. In addition to consulting for USAID, he also consults for the World Bank, the UNDP, and the Inter-American Development Bank. His most recent books are *Elections and Democracy in Central America, Revisited* (1995), co-edited with John Booth, and *Development and Underdevelopment, the Political Economy of Global Inequality* (Third Edition, 2003), co-edited with John Passé-Smith. Many years ago, he served as a Peace Corps volunteer in Costa Rica.

Poverty, Participation, and Democracy

A Global Perspective

I

Introduction

Poor People and Democracy

Anirudh Krishna

Social scientists have steadily believed that democracies will more likely exist in richer rather than poorer countries. Analyses of cross-country data have consistently shown democracy to be more prevalent and more stable in countries that have higher-than-average per capita incomes.[1] Based on these statistical observations, a law-like regularity has been postulated, proposing social prerequisites for democracy, stated in terms of material achievement. Continuing in this vein, a comprehensive analysis concluded that the probability democracy will survive in a country "increases steeply and monotonically as per capita incomes get larger. Indeed, democracy is almost certain to survive in countries with per capita incomes above $4,000." Below this level of per capita income, democracy is considered to be at grave risk: "We have learned that the bonds of poverty are difficult to break, that poverty breeds dictatorships" (Przeworski, et al. 2000: 273, 277).

---

[1] Affirmations include Barro (1997); Bollen and Jackman (1985); Cutwright (1963); Huntington (1984); Lipset (1963, 1994); Lipset, Seong and Torres (1993); Londregan and Poole (1996); Posner (1997); Przeworski et al. (2000); Rueschemeyer, Stephens and Stephens (1992); and Winham (1970). Rare challenges are provided by Arat (1988), Mainwaring and Perez-Linan (2003); Mueller (1992), and O'Donnell (1973), who suggest that the effects of economic advancement can be more varied for democracy.

These expectations are, however, confounded by some recent events. Over the past few decades, democracy has broken out of its erstwhile confines. Today, democracy is no more "the exclusive preserve of wealthy lands," states Karatnycky (2004: 83). "Many poor and developing countries achieve a record of respect for political and civil liberties...the survey data show that there are 38 [democratic] countries with an annual Gross National Income per capita (GNIpc) of US$3,500 or less. Of these [countries], 15 are places where yearly GNIpc is below US$1,500" – that is, less than half the threshold level proposed by Przeworski et al. (2000). Apart from India, where democracy has been in place for more than five decades, countries such as Guatemala, Honduras, Mali, Malawi, and Mozambique also now elect their governments and have gained some degree of experience with democratic rule.

Doubts remain about how firmly democracy's roots will become entrenched within the impoverished soils of these newly entered domains. In Guatemala, Honduras, Mali, Malawi, and Mozambique where, respectively, 56 percent, 53 percent, 63 percent, 65 percent, and 69 percent of all citizens live in poverty, can democracy become the only political game in town?[2]

Most often, this question has been answered negatively. It is a view consistently upheld – an empirical regularity close to a social science law – that the existence of mass poverty poses a substantial challenge to democracy. A number of reasons have been put forward in support of this view, foremost among which relates to the attitudes and behaviors of poor people.

"Only in a wealthy society in which relatively few citizens live at the level of real poverty could there be a situation in which the mass of the population intelligently participate in politics and develop the self-restraint necessary to avoid succumbing to the appeals of irresponsible demagogues," asserted Lipset (1963: 31). Later analysts, examining the interrelationship between democracy and economic development, have predominantly hewed to a pessimistic view about the abilities of poor people to support and take part in democracy.

---

[2] These poverty data are taken from World Bank (2005: 258–9).

The Conventional Wisdom: Poor People Provide Poor Support for Democracy

Because they have very little time and money to spare, it is claimed, poor people are unable and unwilling to take part in democracy. Barro (1996: 24) claimed that democracy is "a sort of luxury good. Rich places consume more democracy because this good is desirable for its own sake." In addition, "Human beings appear to frame their values at least partly in response to what psychologist Abraham Maslow ... termed a 'hierarchy of needs'" Diamond (1992: 126). "With rising incomes, [they] become more willing – and more able – to supplement the necessities of life with luxury goods [such as] democratic governance" (Landa and Kapstein 2001: 269).

Thus, individuals' preferences for democracy are expected to rise together with their incomes. Because "the marginal utility of consumption is lower at higher levels of income" (Przeworski and Limongi 1997: 166), relatively richer individuals are expected to have greater concern for democracy, whereas poorer ones are regarded to be more willing to trade off democracy (and other such "luxuries") for greater material consumption at the present time. "Because the resources of the wealthy are more ample, they do not face the same hard tradeoffs" (Rosenstone and Hansen 1993: 13).[3]

Poor people make poor democrats, according to this hierarchy-of-needs hypothesis. It is only when individuals break out of poverty that they begin to demand a role in and provide support for democracy. Thus, the removal of mass poverty is essential to inculcate within the population the attitudes and behaviors that are supportive of democracy. Economic growth "leads to an increase in the number of individuals with sufficient time, education, and money to get involved in politics" (Bueno de Mesquita and Downs 2005: 79).

Additional arguments have been put forward that further buttress this view. "Extremist and intolerant movements in modern society

---

[3] A variant of this hypothesis, proposing shorter time-horizons for poorer people, is suggested by Varshney (2000: 730): "For the poor, poverty alleviation measures that are direct carry a great deal more weight in the short run than measures that are indirect and have a long-run impact."

are more likely to be based on the lower classes than on the middle and upper classes...the lower class way of life produces individuals with rigid and intolerant approaches to politics...the lower strata are relatively more authoritarian...more attracted to an extremist movement than to a moderate or democratic one...once recruited, they will not be alienated by its lack of democracy, while more educated or sophisticated voters will tend to drop away [from authoritarian movements]....The more well-to-do are more liberal, the poorer are more intolerant" (Lipset 1963: 87, 89, 92). One "should not be upset to learn," claimed (Lipset 1960: 271), "that poverty, insecurity, and ignorance do not produce as 'decent' people as do wealth, security, and knowledge."

Short of money and time, and imbued additionally with the wrong set of values, poor people are presumed to make poor democrats. Similar views, holding out an elite theory of democracy, were also advanced by Schumpeter (1950), and Adorno (1950) equated poverty with an authoritarian personality.

Subsequent arguments about a supposed "culture of poverty" have further tended to bolster the view that poor people are less supportive of democracy. The poor "are a different kind of people," claimed Michael Harrington (1962: 146). "They think and feel differently" from other people. Poverty "is a way of life," declared Oscar Lewis (1963: xxiv), which is "remarkably stable and persistent, passed down from generation to generation along family lines. The culture of poverty has its own modalities and distinctive social and psychological consequences for its members...[it] affects participation in the larger national culture, and becomes a subculture of its own." In particular, the poor are expected to participate much less than others in various democratic activities, constituting an enclave of apathy or – if you believe Adorno and Lipset – actual hostility toward democracy.

As people become richer, their values are supposed to change, becoming increasingly more supportive of democracy. "Democracy has an intrinsic value that is increasingly sought after as populations become better off" (Helliwell 1994: 246). "Economic development is linked with coherent, and to some extent predictable, changes in culture and social and political life....Industrialization leads to... broader political participation and less easily led publics" (Inglehart and Baker 2000: 21). "Rising levels of existential security and auto-nomy change people's firsthand life experiences fundamentally, lead-ing them to emphasize goals that were previously given low prior-ity, including the pursuit of freedom.... [These changed] values bring increasing emphasis on the civil and political liberties that constitute democracy" (Inglehart and Welzel 2005: 2–3).

Different traditions of research – including rational choice, encap-sulated in the hierarchy-of-needs hypothesis, but also political cul-ture approaches – have commonly arrived at the same conclusion: poorer people make less reliable democrats than richer ones. Democ-racy is therefore not expected to become firmly entrenched until people become richer and a substantial middle class takes shape.

Poor people living in rural areas are expected to be especially worse off in this regard. Although the depiction of the *urban* working class as apathetic or hostile has been stridently challenged – with Rueschmeyer, Stephens, and Stephens (1992: 8) labeling this group as "the most consistently pro-democratic force" – no similar contentions have been expressed about the poor in rural areas. "The rural population," stated Lipset (1963: 105), "both farmers and laborers, tends to oppose civil liberties and multi-party systems more than any other occupational group." Additionally, "The secular evolution of a participant society appears to involve a regular sequence of phases. Urbanization comes first," asserted Lerner (1958: 60), on whose work Lipset drew to a considerable extent.

Participation in democracy is thus expected to be especially unlikely in rural areas. Small farmers or rural laborers, who constitute the bulk of the poor in South Asia, and self-provisioning peasants, constitut-ing most of the poor in Sub-Saharan Africa, are considered in the conventional wisdom as least likely to come out in support of democ-racy. "The people of poor societies and societies with high percentages working in the agrarian sector tend to hold traditional values, while the people of richer societies with a higher percentage of the labor force in the industrial sector tend to hold secular – rational values" (Inglehart and Baker 2000: 38). Traditional values, it must be remembered, are supposed to be antithetical to democracy. Thus countries where large numbers of people are in the agrarian sector – and poor to boot – are the ones in which democracy is least likely to gain mass support.

The prognosis for the new democracies of the South is therefore grim, according to these views. Most individuals in these countries are not expected to be particularly democratic in their attitudes and behaviors. Lack of time and lack of money, along with a particular set of values associated with this lifestyle, are expected to diminish support and deter mass participation in democracy. Support for democracy, if there is any, is likely to be confined within a relatively small group of westernized city-based elites, who have ascended to middle-class status, acquiring values associated with urbanization, industrialization, and exposure to mass media. The essays in this volume show that the truth is much less clear cut.

Empirical Holes in the Conventional Vision

Although it has held sway for a very long time, there is a stunning lack of supportive empirical evidence for the conventional wisdom. Analyses supporting such conclusions have *not* directly demonstrated that poor people in poor countries in fact show little support for democracy.

Empirical evidence has been provided demonstrating that at any given point in time poor *countries* are less likely to be democratic than richer ones. Evidence has also been advanced showing that poor people in *rich* countries participate in democracy at a lower level than their fellow citizens.[4] But it is only a stretch of the imagination that extends these arguments to apply to poor people in poorer countries.

Most analysts, including Lipset, have relied on aggregate, that is, country-level and cross-sectional, data. Conclusions about individual behavior are both assumed in and derived from these aggregate-level analyses. Thus, for example, Bilson (1982: 103), after analyzing differences across countries, nevertheless feels prompted to predict for the individual level "a positive correlation between freedom and real income. On the demand side, freedom must be considered a luxury good so that the resources devoted to the attainment of individual freedom are likely to be greater when per capita income is high. On

---

[4] Including Almond and Verba (1965); Jackman (1987); Jackman and Miller (1995); Lijphart (1997); Powell (1982); Rosenstone and Hansen (1993); Verba, Nie, and Kim (1978); Verba, Schlozman, and Brady (1995); and Wolfinger and Rosenstone (1980).

the supply side, it is undoubtedly more costly to repress a wealthy person than a poor person and the need to do so is probably less acute."

Using aggregate data does not make clear whether the regularities observed in the past at the country level will necessarily continue into the future. Although statistical analyses have been consistent in showing that at any given point in time democracy tends to be stronger in richer rather than poorer countries, it does not follow that as any particular country becomes richer, it will also simultaneously *become* more democratic. In fact, Arat's (1988: 33–34) longitudinal analysis "yields widely varying relationships between levels of socioeconomic development and democracy . . . [showing that] democracy is not a one-way ladder that countries climb" as their economy expands.

Even though the data do not make clear what governments and concerned others should do in order to support democracy in the future, analysts holding the conventional view have been hardly shy about proposing programs of action that would, in effect, deny democracy to people in poor countries – or at least, withhold it until mass poverty was removed. For example, Barro (1996: 24) proposes that "the advanced [W]estern countries would contribute more to the welfare of poor nations by exporting their economic systems, notably property rights and free markets, rather than their political systems, which typically developed after reasonable standards of living had been attained. If economic freedom can be established in a poor country, then growth would be encouraged, and the country would tend eventually to become more democratic on its own. Thus, in the long run, the propagation of Western-style economic systems would also be the more effective way to expand democracy in the world."

Apart from the lack of any clear causal framework, the lack of robust micro-foundations makes any such argument deeply suspect. No evidence is available to show whether and how poor individuals in poor democracies care any more or less for democracy than their richer counterparts. "The relation between the 'macro' socioeconomic changes and the 'macro' political change has to be mediated through 'micro' changes in the attitudes, values and behavior of individuals. The [lack of] explanation of the latter is the weak link in the causal change that is assumed to exist," stated Huntington (1971: 310).

Neither the hierarchy-of-needs hypothesis nor culture-based arguments have been empirically tested at the individual level within developing country contexts, especially not after the establishment of democracy in these countries.[5] Within industrialized democracies, surveys have shown repeatedly that poor people participate less vigorously than others in democracy – particularly in its "more intensive and time-consuming forms" (Lijphart 1997: 1), such as contacting, organizing, demonstrating, and protesting – and this evidence regarding lower participation levels among poorer people in the West has been projected uncritically to posit a lower general regard for democracy in countries where large numbers of people are poor.

Even as the third and fourth wave of democracies became established in Asia, Africa and Latin America, this conventional wisdom has held sway, albeit without firm empirical underpinnings. The key anomalous case of India, for decades among the world's poorest nations, but also among the most resilient democracies, has often been brushed aside, or explained away as a legacy of the British colonial tradition (Bollen and Jackman 1985; Lipset, Seong, and Torres 1993), even though that same tradition did not yield democracy in many other settings.

It is time, therefore, to subject the conventional wisdom to systematic empirical testing. If democracy were, indeed, a luxury good, as stated in these arguments, valued and practiced by richer more than poorer individuals, then one would expect to find systematic differences in average levels of democratic attitudes and behavior. Within each country, people with higher incomes should exhibit significantly greater support for democracy, *and* their levels of participation in various democratic activities, particularly the more time-consuming

---

[5] Inglehart and Welzel (2005: 233–4), although collecting data at the individual level and framing their hypotheses in terms of individuals' motivations and values, nevertheless expect their conclusions about value change to operate exclusively at the aggregate national level. They hold that "aggregate data represent mass tendencies that are almost exogenous to each of the individuals from which they are calculated." However, they do not explain at what particular level of aggregation – locality, district, province, or region – these mass tendencies begin to make themselves manifest. Why should it occur only at the level of the nation – a recent, incomplete, and often, an artificial construct in many non-Western contexts?

ones, should be systematically greater than those of poorer individuals. And if cultural values were, in fact, systematically different among relatively poorer and relatively richer individuals, with some nonparticipative culture of poverty being particularly embedded within the former group, then levels of support and participation rates should diverge further across income groups. An extensive empirical examination, spanning twenty-four countries and more than thirty thousand individual interviews, reveals that these expectations are hardly justified.

The Argument in this Book: Poor People Are *Not* Less Democratic

The essays in this volume present the first set of robust empirical results from a geographically diverse selection of countries spanning three continents. The authors take advantage of the globalization of public attitude survey research that has followed in the wake of democratic transitions in developing countries (Heath, Fisher, and Smith 2005). Undertaken independently of each other, with no prior knowledge or communication among the researchers concerned, these studies nevertheless report a striking common conclusion.

The conventional wisdom, these studies uniformly find, is *wrong* – or at least, if ever correct, it is no longer true. In countries of Africa, Latin America, and South Asia, poor people do not value democracy any less than their richer counterparts. Their faith in democracy is as high as (and sometimes higher than) other citizens', and they participate in democratic activities no less (and sometimes more) than other citizens. These results are empirically robust, geographically widespread, and they provide new and exciting grounds for optimism regarding the future of democracy.

Democracy is widely welcomed in the new domains where it has been introduced. By large majorities, both rich and poor citizens prefer democracy to alternative forms of government, and they turn up in large numbers to participate in various democratic activities.

Social science theories tend to seriously underpredict the vast mass of support for democracy observed among poor people in poor countries. Neither rational choice nor culture-based arguments predict well the actual attitudes and behaviors reported by thousands of individuals, relatively rich and relatively poor, who were interviewed for the separate research projects reported in this book.

An earlier empirical examination undertaken in India showed that poor people and those with lower social status voted in significantly larger numbers compared with their richer counterparts (Yadav 1999, 2000). Examining voting behavior, Yadav (1999: 2397) concluded that the "textbook rule about political participation is that the higher you are in the social hierarchy, the greater the chance of your participating in political activity, including voting.... India is perhaps the only exception to this rule.... The continuous influx of people increasingly from the lower orders of society in the arena of democratic contestation provides the setting, the stimuli, and the limits to how the election system unfolds." The evidence presented here extends this conclusion to different countries, showing that India is not the only exception to the putative "textbook rule."

The data examined here show that poor people's positive affinity for democracy is by no means confined to voting. People can vote for a variety of reasons, and if the cynics have it right, poor people might even on occasion be paid to cast their votes. It is found, however, that in terms of a vast variety of engagements with democracy – including campaigning, contacting, protesting, and other time- and resource-intensive forms – poorer people are hardly behind richer ones, and in many instances they are even ahead by a significant distance.

Neither participation nor faith in democracy suffers on account of individual poverty. Poor citizens participate equally vigorously in a plethora of democratic activities. It stands to reason that they should do so; democracy provides an avenue that poor people can utilize for overcoming generations of domination or neglect.

In chapter 2, Michael Bratton examines data from a series of recent Afrobarometer surveys for fifteen countries in sub-Saharan Africa, countries that are among the poorest in the world, with large parts of the population residing in rural areas, mostly self-provisioning peasants following an agrarian lifestyle. He finds a "clear absence of any anti-democracy constituency among the African poor." People at all levels of material well-being tend to have nearly similar views on political tolerance, political accountability, and political equality. In terms of behaviors, poor people in these countries, even very poor ones, vote more frequently than richer ones, and they are also more likely than others to participate in various political activities between elections.

Similar results for rural India are presented by Krishna in Chapter 3. Interviewing a random sample of more than two thousand individuals, residents of sixty-one north Indian villages, in 1997 and again in 2004, Krishna finds that faith in democracy is not significantly different across different wealth categories. Poorer as well as richer villagers express themselves strongly in support of democracy. Political efficacy and political participation levels are also not significantly influenced by differences in individuals' wealth. Neither individuals' current levels of material well-being nor their well-being levels seven years ago help explain who participates in various acts associated with making democracy work better.

In chapter 4, Booth and Seligson examine recent survey data from eight Latin American countries. Conducting interviews with 1,500 individuals in each of these countries, selected through a process of stratified random sampling, with special care taken to ensure the representation of the rural poor, they find that individual wealth has no perceptible association with voting, party and campaign activism, communal activism, civil society engagement, or protest participation. Wealth is significantly associated with one aspect of participation – contacting public officials – but it is negatively rather than positively related: poor people are more active than others in contacting officials. Booth and Seligson also present results from a parallel set of analyses undertaken for the aggregate, national level. Per capita income, they find, not significantly related to any of six different aspects of participation. They further find that personal wealth and aggregate-level wealth have no significant impact on preference for elected government or basic democratic norms.

Thus, individual-level as well as national-level examinations point to the same overall conclusion: poverty in Latin America is not a valid predictor, in general, of support for democracy or participation levels.[6]

---

[6] Employing a different aggregate-level data set, Mainwaring and Perez-Linan (2003: 131) find similarly that "Democracy in Latin America has survived in the face of a low level of [economic] development, and it has faltered despite moderately high per capita income."

Taken together, these three sets of analyses, which collectively cover a total of twenty-four countries in Africa, Asia, and Latin America, including individual interviews with more than 35,000 respondents, demonstrate that *democracy is widely supported by poor people in poor countries*. Democracy in poor countries is not likely to become unstable because of lack of support among poor people. Poor people in these countries are not disengaged, apathetic, or averse to democratic governance in their countries. On the contrary, they express themselves staunchly in support of democracy compared to all other alternatives, and they participate no less than their richer counterparts in various activities associated with making democracy work.

Was the conventional wisdom always wrong in relation to the democracies of the South, or have some things changed fundamentally in recent years, altering the individual-level relationship between wealth and democracy? Two factors have changed critically. First, the expansion of education, especially within rural areas and poorer sections of the population, has considerably widened and deepened the base of support for democracy. Second, simultaneously, there has been a broad diffusion, nationally and internationally, of a normative basis of support for democracy: "It is becoming both uncouth and unprofitable to avoid free elections" (Lipset 1994: 16).

It is possible that the conventional wisdom might have been challenged even earlier. However, persistent data gaps have so far stood in the way. Because, individual-level data on poverty are still not readily available within developing countries, analysts have relied on aggregate national-level statistics, and they have projected their conclusions, wrongly, as it turns out, to apply as well to poor *people* in poorer countries. Individual-level data need to be collected afresh so that links with democracy at this level can be directly explored.

The authors in this volume have constructed innovative measures of relative wealth, and they have utilized these measures to assess wealth levels for thousands of individuals selected through random sampling. Utilized in conjunction with surveys of political attitudes, values, and behavior, these individual-level wealth measures have yielded the important new results reported in this volume. These methodological developments are worth noting, along with the conclusions that these studies report. Bratton and colleagues have developed a Lived Poverty

Index based on access, or lack thereof, to basic human needs among the African populations they have surveyed. Krishna has come up with the Stages-of-Progress methodology, which he utilized for investigations not only in rural India but also separately in Kenya, Uganda, Peru, and North Carolina in the United States.[7] Booth and Seligson utilized an index of assets to gauge relative wealth in the Latin American contexts that they studied. These measures have assisted to a considerable extent in filling the empirical gaps that have remained large, playing a major role in leading the conventional wisdom astray.

Education and Information Matter More than Wealth

Another conclusion that these three studies commonly reach relates to the value added by education for both participation and faith in democracy. Although wealth is not in the most part related to political values and political behaviors, education is strongly and commonly associated with increased support and enhanced participation. In general, people who are more educated participate relatively more often in various democratic activities, and they also show stronger support for democracy.

As education is spreading fast, especially among poorer and more rural communities that were hitherto rarely provided with teachers and schools, a new generation is taking over, composed of educated younger peasants and educated poor people in cities. Democracy is especially strongly supported within this cohort of people, growing rapidly across most of the developing world.

Analyses of democratic engagement conducted in rich democracies have shown that education matters separately from wealth (Jackson 1995; Nie, Junn and Stehlik-Barry 1996, Sullivan and Transue 1999; Wolfinger and Rosenstone 1980). Individual-level data on education and wealth have been available for these Western contexts, and they show that education and wealth are often unaligned, with poorer individuals also acquiring at least some amount of high school education.

---

7 Citations to published papers and copies of working papers along with details of the Stages of Progress methodology are available at www.pubpol.duke.edu/krishna

This availability of micro-level data has made it possible to analyze within richer countries the separate effects of education and wealth.

Similar analyses are now possible for the Third World. More young-sters going to school in ever-increasing numbers have pushed up the average literacy figures for entire countries. Just over the past decade, "literacy levels in developing countries have increased from 70 percent to 76 percent" (UNDP 2005: 20), and this pace of increase continues unabated.

These trends are particularly visible within the younger cohorts in developing countries – and they are hardly confined to a richer subset of people. Surveys conducted on behalf of the World Bank between 2003 and 2005 show that among Kenyans ages fifteen to nineteen years old, more than 75 percent of the poorest 40 percent (and about 90 percent of the richest 20 percent) had completed Grade 5. In Bolivia, within the same age group, a little less than 85 percent of the poorest 40 percent and about 95 percent of the richest 20 percent had completed Grade 5. The comparable figures for Peru show that there is no difference between the poorest 40 percent and the richest 20 percent, with 90 per-cent of both cohorts having completed Grade 5. For Malawi, the dif-ference between the poor and the rich is larger: 60 percent of the poorest 40 percent and 80 percent of the richest 20 percent ages fifteen to nineteen years had completed Grade 5.

The remaining disparities between rich and poor are growing even smaller as more and more children go to school. Among ten-year-olds, more than 85 percent of the poorest 40 percent in Malawi (and 95 per-cent of the richest 20 percent) are currently enrolled in school. In Peru, there is virtually no difference in this regard across wealth cate-gories: more than 95 percent of all ten-year-olds, both rich and poor, are enrolled in school. In Kenya as well, there is virtually no differ-ence across these wealth categories, with 90-plus percent commonly enrolled in schools.[8]

Of course, the quality of schooling might (and most likely will) differ across wealth categories, and of course, children who are richer will most likely continue in school for a longer time. But the point is that the

---

[8] These data are available at www.worldbank.org/research/projects/edattain

illiterate peasant is increasingly becoming a thing of the past. Education among the poor of developing countries is much higher for the younger generation compared with their mothers and fathers and especially with their grandmothers and grandfathers.[9] And this acquisition of the ability to read and write gives to these younger generations of poorer people a greater ability than their forebears to negotiate and make sense of the written world, a world in which both contemporary states and markets operate. Previously mostly impenetrable by poor people, democracy is now better understood by them, and they can be better engaged with it.

Bratton, in his analysis of sub-Saharan Africa, finds that as people accumulate years of schooling, they become ever more likely to prefer democracy and to reject authoritarian alternatives. At a time when poorer as well as richer villagers are increasingly going to school, the base of support for African democracy is expanding steadily. In a related study, Evans and Rose (2007) contend that, even when raised under authoritarian rule and lacking access to adult civic education, educated people "have a firmer grasp on meaning: not only do they support democracy but they have a better understanding of why they are supporting it." Moreover, primary schooling – the modal educational experience of African citizens – has a strong positive effect on general preferences for democracy and rejection of non-democratic alternatives.

In this volume, Krishna's chapter shows that in rural north India, education is consistently positively associated with both political efficacy and political participation. The correlation coefficient between education and wealth is getting reduced, because poorer as well as richer villagers, especially younger ones, are entering schools in ever-increasing numbers. Educated villagers are expanding the scope of their engagements in the public realm. Their reach is no longer confined to

---

[9] Krishna (2003) provides a comparative analysis of educational attainment across age groups for a sample of residents in sixty villages of north India, showing that while they were previously closely aligned, education and wealth are no longer closely associated within north Indian villages. As schools have expanded into even quite remote rural areas over the past twenty-five years, poorer villagers are increasingly acquiring functional literacy, and the educational gap across wealth categories is closing rapidly.

the strongman in their village. Their newfound abilities let them reach out farther, making more numerous and more diverse contacts with public officials and party organizers (Krishna 2002, 2003).

In Latin America as well, Booth and Seligson find that a variable for years of education is consistently associated with individuals' engagements with democracy. More generally, education is closely related to a battery of outcomes associated with strengthening and broad-basing support for democracy. Progressively higher levels of education tend to raise both participation and support for democracy, but in relatively small increments.[10]

Education, even primary education, is a powerful resource for participation in democracy. Information, considered separately by Krishna in chapter 3, is an equally powerful resource. Measured in terms of the number of different information sources (out of a total of eight) that a respondent consulted over the thirty-day-period prior to the interview, the variable for information is strongly positively associated with political participation as well as political efficacy.

Similar results regarding the value to democracy of education are also reported in some recent aggregate-level analyses. Modeling democratic transitions and stability for the longer period, 1850–1990, Boix and Stokes (2003: 543; emphasis added) find that the "statistical significance of per capita income . . . is *strongly eroded* by the introduction of the index of education." Przeworski et al. (2000: 137; emphasis added) – who also posit an income threshold below which democracy is unlikely to survive –remark that "Education helps [democracies] to survive *independently* of income." Thus, democracy can be stabilized even when the income threshold is not crossed, provided that education is sufficiently expanded.

---

[10] Once populations become largely school-going, the incremental effects on participation of additional years of school are somewhat modest. In Latin America, where the rate of literacy has been comparatively greater for a longer time, such modest incremental effects are demonstrated by Booth and Seligson in chapter 4. Much larger effects are experienced in India and sub-Saharan Africa, however, where a surge in school-going has been more recently experienced and comparatively larger proportions of the population, especially older folk, continue to remain illiterate. Evidence from the United States also indicates that diminishing returns might set in when levels of education become relatively high on average. See for instance Davis (1998) and Nie et al. (1996).

Expanding education helps stabilize democracy. Becoming a democrat is a cognitive learning process, as Bratton states in his chapter. Education and information help people become better democrats; wealth is mostly inconsequential to this process. The conventional wisdom is, therefore, right in one key respect: socioeconomic characteristics do matter, but it is not wealth so much as education that provides the bedrock of mass support for democracy. It is not only the middle class but also educated peasants and slum dwellers who make up the ranks of committed and engaged democratic citizens.

Is Democracy Safe?

Do poor people make good democrats? The conclusions reported in chapters 2, 3, and 4 would appear to suggest that the answer is, by and large, a resounding "Yes." The future of democracy is not under threat because of lack of support among poor people in poor countries.

But could it be that democracy is still under threat in these countries either despite – or more worryingly, because of – what poor people feel about democracy? Establishing that poor people strongly support democracy does not amount to showing that democracy is itself firmly established. Alternative scenarios presented in different parts of the literature indicate possibilities for democratic reversal that will need to be separately addressed. Will poor people, now strongly in support, begin to abjure democracy in the future if their economic demands remain largely unfulfilled? Are rising and uncontainable economic demands from newly mobilized poor people likely to submerge the capacities of fledgling democracies, resulting in ungovernability and possibly a retreat from democracy (Huntington 1968; Huntington and Nelson 1976)? How likely is it that fears of redistributive demands from democratically mobilized poor people will tempt elites in these countries to suspend or roll back democracy (Acemoglu and Robinson 2006; Boix 2003)?

These fears of democratic reversals give reason for concern; they cannot be entirely denied – or confirmed – given the evidence at hand. Yes, democracies in poorer countries can be – and have been – reversed; thus, it is prudent to work unremittingly toward their further consolidation and institutionalization, as Przeworski advises in chapter 5 of this volume. But civil and political rights in much richer democracies have also been repealed or suspended or surreptitiously whittled away at times. So nurturing democracy and protecting individual rights vigilantly is a crucial task in rich as well as poor democracies. If there is some particular weakness in the newer and poorer democracies, it arises, in my view and Przeworski's (in chapter 5), from the embryonic nature of political and civic institutions in many of these countries. Strengthening institutions – such as courts, political parties, and a free and active media – provides ordinary citizens with greater protections and is an important remaining task for stabilizing democracy in these countries.

Thus, although remaining optimistic and vigilant, one must be cautious about the survival and consolidation of democracy in poor countries. Some comments on the hypotheses expressed earlier are nevertheless still in order; some insights from this volume speak directly to these hypotheses.

First, there is the hypothesis that poor people might turn against democracy if their economic demands are not amply fulfilled. An important assumption underlying this hypothesis – as well as the one related to elites' fear of redistributive demands – is that individuals' concerns for democracies are instrumental and not intrinsic; people tend to trade-off democracy against their own economic well-being. Thus, people who feel that democracy will more likely help improve their economic situations are assumed to have a positive preference for democracy, whereas those who fear its consequences for their pocketbooks are assumed to have the opposite preference. These assumptions imply that people cannot have a preference for democracy *independent* of its expected economic consequences; they do not value democracy for and of itself. Apart from leading to a logical conundrum,[11] this assumption, inherent in most rational-choice explanations, is also not verified by the data examined in this volume.

---

[11] Hewing closely to the economic logic makes us prisoner to the following conundrum: A rational person cares more for democracy if it raises his or her income, but a rational person also finds it irrational to vote. Unless people think extra-rationally, therefore, there will be no voters and no democracy. But if they think extra-rationally, then income may not be all they will consider while evaluating their preference for democracy or dictatorship.

Bratton demonstrates in chapter 2 that even though poor people feel – in larger numbers compared to richer ones – that democracy has so far mostly failed them in regard to socioeconomic development, they nevertheless tend to strongly reject all nondemocratic alternatives, including military rule, one-person rule, and one-party rule. "Poor people in Africa will not easily surrender their voting rights and may sometimes even use these rights to discipline poorly performing leaders." In a head-to-head comparison of these different motivations, he found more intrinsic compared to instrumental support for democracy: 50 percent thought that democracy is worth having simply because it allows a popular voice in decision making versus 38 percent who insisted that democracy must address everyone's basic material needs. To be sure, richer people were significantly more likely to view democracy intrinsically. But almost half of all poorer Africans expressed an intrinsic appreciation of democracy, which is a greater proportion than those who viewed democracy instrumentally.

A similar result is provided by a recent survey of more than 35,000 adults selected in eight West African capital cities together with more than 50,000 individuals interviewed in four Latin American countries.

While 31 percent of all respondents stated that the economic system does not work well in a democracy and over one-third considered that democracies have problems maintaining order, these shortcomings were minor compared to the advantages that people saw of democracy. Over 80 percent of people were convinced that, all things considered, democracy – understood as a political process for selecting leaders via the ballot box – is still the best system compared to other forms of government. (Herrera, Razafindrakoto, and Roubaud 2006: 48)

It is also important to remember that hard times (or good times) overall do not affect all poor (or rich) individuals equally. A rising tide that lifts all boats is clearly a myth, hardly ever experienced in practice. Investigations of the intertemporal economic fates of different households show clearly that during any given period of time some households rise while others fall into poverty (Krishna 2006a). Thus, no matter how well or how poorly the national economy is doing overall, some individuals always fare poorly, and many actually become impoverished.

Are the individuals who suffer a reversal in fortune more likely than others to lose support for democracy? Krishna provides some evidence in chapter 3 that has the effect of allaying these fears to some extent. His two-period data base – interviewing nearly two thousand individuals in both 1997 and 2004 – identifies those individuals who suffered economic reverses and actually fell into poverty during these seven years. He finds that the level of support for democracy among this subgroup of people is not significantly different than the levels of other subgroups. People who fell into poverty do not blame democracy for their misfortunes.

People, including poor people, are becoming sophisticated enough to differentiate between democracy (as a system of rule) and the government presently in power. Krishna finds in rural India that although "democracy is supported by the vast majority of villagers, rich and poor alike... there is widespread cynicism about government agents' performance on a day-to-day basis." Similarly, Bratton and Mattes (2001a: 108) draw a sharp distinction between support for democracy and satisfaction with economic results, finding that "survey respondents support democracy even when dissatisfied with [the government's] capacity to deliver."

A further confirmation that the poor are not disproportionately unsupportive of democracy is seen in Booth and Seligson's finding that no significant relationship exists between levels of personal wealth and either support for fundamental democratic norms or a preference for elected leaders over unelected strongman leaders. Even controlling for education, community size, national context, and legitimacy norms, the poor do not differ significantly from the wealthy in these democratic attitudes. This calls seriously into question the idea that working class authoritarianism might threaten democracy, at least in these eight Latin American nations.

There are indications, thus, that people in these countries value democracy as much or more for intrinsic rather than instrumental reasons. Considering parallel changes in the international normative context, Lipset (1994: 2) partially revises his earlier position, holding that democracy may not be so much "a 'rational choice,' particularly in the new, less stable, less legitimate polities." A strengthening normative basis of support is taking hold, he suggests, making democracy both an international cause and a national imperative. Diamond (1992: 102) refers similarly to a "globalization of democracy, in terms of the near-universalization of popular demands for political freedom, representation, participation, and accountability."

The authors in this volume find these effects echoed within the rural and urban communities that they have studied in different developing countries. People value democracy more for what it is politically and institutionally than for what it does economically for them. It seems unlikely, therefore, that poor people will lose support for democracy – as a system of government – just because the government of the day fails to meet their material demands. Nevertheless, creating institutions that enable these demands to be channeled in orderly fashion, while respecting the rights of other citizens, remains very important, much as Huntington (1968) observed forty years ago.

What of the second argument? Do elites, instead, support democracy only insofar as their wealth is not threatened by redistributive demands emanating from mobilized poor people? And will they be willing and able to subvert democracy when they feel these threats are growing too large?

Let us take note first that a distinction needs to be made between poverty, on the one hand, and inequality, on the other. Muller (1988: 66; emphasis in original) finds that "a very strong inverse association is observed between income inequality and the likelihood of stability versus breakdown of democracy. . . . [But] this negative effect of income inequality on democratic stability is *independent* of a country's level of economic development." Mass poverty is not the factor that tends to jeopardize democracy in this argument – though it can exacerbate these effects, as pointed out by Przeworski in chapter 5 – however, it is inequality that initially moves elites to fear, and on occasion, to subvert democracy. "In highly unequal societies," as Boix (2003: 3) puts it, "the redistributive demands of the worse-off citizens on the wealthy are particularly intense. As a result, the latter have a strong incentive to oppose the introduction of democracy, which would enable the majority to impose heavy taxes on them."[12]

---

[12] The connection with economic development is made by Boix on account of the fact that broadly, over a long historical period, economic growth has, in general, gone

How real are these fears?[13] Unfortunately, authors who set forth the inequality-redistribution argument – Boix (2003) as much as Acemoglu and Robinson (2006) – provide "no systematic evidence on how the structural variables of inequality and asset specificity play themselves out with real actors, which is where the causal action is said to lie" (Ziblatt 2006: 322). Even though two micro-level assumptions underpin the inequality-redistribution argument – (a) that poor people have systematically stronger preferences for democracy than their richer counterparts, and (b) that rich people's preferences for democracy are, in fact, weaker in societies that have significantly higher levels of inequality – no micro-level evidence is provided related to these assumed preferences and behaviors.

Micro-level evidence examined here provides support for neither assumption. First, individual wealth is mostly *not* significant in

together with reduced inequality. In his scheme, the prevalence of highly immobile forms of capital such as land exacerbates the probability of the authoritarian solution. Long-term economic growth, by simultaneously both reducing inequality and enhancing elites' ownership of assets that are comparatively more mobile, that is, financial rather than physical assets, tends to reduce fears of redistribution among elites, thereby lowering their incentives for imposing authoritarian remedies.

[13] It is curious to note that challenges to the probable coexistence of mass poverty and democracy rely not on any single set of assumptions but on two diametrically opposed sets. The original Lipset hypothesis, recall, was based on the assumption that the poor have no great concern for democracy; authoritarian tendencies associated with the lower classes tend to make their numbers inimical to democracy. The inequality-redistribution arguments turn this assumption on its head. Here it is assumed that poor people are inherently *more* democratic than rich elites. "Where does the demand for democracy come from" in these arguments, asks Ziblatt (2006: 317)? Implicitly, it "*always* emerges 'from below.'" Thus, whether the poor are assumed to stay distant from democracy (as in the Lipset hypothesis) or whether they are assumed to hold it close (as in the inequality–redistribution arguments), the presence of large numbers of poor people is presumed to have the same ultimate effect: mass poverty is regarded as detrimental to democratic stability, no matter what poor people believe and how they act! Clearly, the Lipset hypothesis and the inequality-redistribution hypothesis cannot both be simultaneously true; if both were true, that would imply that poor people's attitudes and actions did not matter in the least, and if these attitudes and actions do not matter, then it makes no difference how many poor people live within a country; democracy would have no palpable relationship with the level of economic development. In order to continue proposing the adverse connection between poverty and democracy, either one or both of these hypotheses has to be dismissed as incorrect.

analyses of democratic values, political efficacy, or political participation. Thus, although poor people are not less democratic than richer ones, neither are they consistently and strongly more pro-democracy.

Second, among the subset of richer people interviewed, attitudes and practices are not significantly different across societies that have varying levels of inequality. Krishna undertakes these comparisons across the sixty-one rural communities that he examines, finding that within-community levels of inequality are not significantly related to across-community differences in faith for democracy. People (specifically, richer people) do not express less faith in democracy in communities where inequality is higher. Conducting a similar analysis, Booth and Seligson show that a higher Gini coefficient goes together at the country level in Latin America with a slightly lower overall support for democracy, indicating that greater inequality is associated with less support for democracy. However, their variable for wealth does not correlate significantly with support for democracy, either at the country level or at the individual level, suggesting that it is not particularly the rich in these countries who are fearful of democracy's consequences. Bratton finds for sub-Saharan Africa that the connection between support for democracy (aggregated at the country level) and an inequality ratio (of the richest: poorest quintiles' share of income) is neither strong nor statistically significant.[14]

Our data do not, therefore, provide much empirical support for the individual-level assumptions inherent in these inequality – redistribution arguments. However, they also do not entirely remove the disquiet engendered by these arguments.

Apprehensions about instability on account of elite reactions remain. It is possible, for example, that elites, presently strongly pro-democracy, might be led in the future to believe, quite likely at the urging of some demagogues among them – for how else would they collectively gain a call to urgent action? – that all was not well with democracy, and rising demands by the poor for education, employment, and entitlements threatened to upend their well-filled nests. It is also possible that populist administrations that meet (and sometimes

---

[14] Personal communication from Michael Bratton.

exceed) the demands made by poor people might continue deriving
support, at least ostensibly, even after they take an authoritarian turn.
Contemporary Venezuela is cited in this context by Booth and Seligson
in chapter 4 of this volume. Some clouds remain, therefore, as concerns
the future of democracy, as Przeworski remarks in chapter 5.

Building strong institutions is particularly important in this regard.
Institutions that can deter potential authoritarians and their supporters
while enforcing fair and equitable processes will help entrench people's
intrinsic support for democracy. It is significant to note that the longer
a democracy survives the more likely it is, by and large, to become
more strongly democratic. Booth and Seligson show that the longevity
of democracy is positively correlated with many democratic behaviors.
These positive effects also spill over to infect other countries of the
region (Bernhard, Nordstrom, and Reenock 2001). Democratization
in the neighborhood has a strong demonstration effect (Gasiorowski
1995). As the new democracies acquire a stronger basis in institutions, the already strong public support for them should become
even stronger, possibly also spilling over to other countries in their
vicinity.

Consolidating Democracy in Poorer Countries

Three related elements are mentioned by Linz and Stepan (1996) as
being associated with and responsible for the consolidation of democracy: *Behaviorally*, no significant actor in the country spends significant resources attempting to achieve their objectives by creating a
nondemocratic alternative or by seceding from the democratic state.
Attitudinally, a strong majority of people hold the belief that democratic procedures and institutions are the most appropriate way to
govern collective life in a society such as theirs, and support for anti-
system alternatives is quite small. *Constitutionally*, governmental and
nongovernmental forces alike become habituated to the resolution of
conflict within specified institutions and procedures sanctioned by the
new democratic process.

The evidence presented in this volume shows that, in terms of the
attitudinal element, opportunities are present for regime consolidation

in the new democracies of Africa and Latin America. Indeed, this outcome may already have come to pass in parts of rural India.

Behaviorally, as well, neither poorer nor richer citizens of these countries appear to be investing in promoting non-democratic alternatives or seceding from their democratic states. People here participate in large numbers in various activities associated with making democracy work, and these figures for participation are larger in comparison to those reported for richer and longer-standing democracies.

Still, all is not as well as it should be. Bratton in Chapter 2 of this volume finds that commitments to democracy, although widespread, continue to be somewhat shallow and tentative in Africa. Access – to the protections, benefits, and opportunities of democracy – continues to remain a significant problem, especially for poorer people and those who live in more remote areas. "The central state remains a relatively remote and inaccessible apparatus to most Africans." Although political parties remain weak and not highly trusted, they are still capable of mobilizing poorer Africans to vote, especially in rural areas. At the same time, poor rural dwellers continue to direct their political demands most often along informal channels, relying on traditional authorities, religious leaders, and other local notables. Krishna finds that individuals who feel excluded because of lack of access are likely to experience a lower sense of personal efficacy; their participation scores are also lower than those of others. Political parties and other intermediate institutions – such as local governments, nongovernmental organizations (NGOs), and other civil society organizations – do not provide most people with a viable avenue for upward representation.

Increasing access to the agencies and institutions that uphold the protections, opportunities, and benefits of democracy is critically important for enhancing people's commitments to democracy. In addition to the national institutions that are usually mentioned in discussions about consolidation, it is equally important in developing country contexts to build and strengthen the intermediate – or middle-level – institutions that enable individual citizens to develop more regular and reliable links with elected representatives and other officials.

Herrera et al. (2006: 57), after surveying the opinions of people in eight West African cities, state that "the populations who tend to be excluded from the social body express high expectations and count explicitly on greater democracy, with its underlying principles of equality before the law and equal opportunities." Institutions that better enable these principles to be converted into practice need to be designed and installed with urgency in developing countries.

Thus, in terms of the third element of consolidating democracy – promoting institutions and procedures sanctioned by the new democratic process – the task remains one of engineering institutions that can help serve this objective within the *specific* contexts of different developing countries. National, as well as middle-level institutions, will need to be designed and installed.

Social democratic parties in Western Europe helped provide the institutional scaffolding for serving poor people's aspirations while directing their demands along democratic avenues. It is likely that some similar and some different designs will emerge in different countries. Hagopian (2000: 902) observes that "countries are not on the path toward a single type of democracy, but an amazing plurality of forms [is emerging. We]...should expect to see appear in societies with similar productive structures and social influences diverse degrees of political centralization, patterns of state strength, and institutional design."

Developing different institutional designs, better suited to securing the gains of democracy for poorer people in different countries, is a critical remaining task for analysts and policymakers alike. Social scientists and others have worried about making democracy more secure. But making democracy more democratic – with its protections and benefits more easily accessed by marginalized people – is as important a task, which needs more attention in the future. We speak to this concern in the concluding chapter of this volume.

Some things have changed from the past that enable greater confidence to be reposed in the prospects for democracy in poor countries. Increasing education has assisted in more widely spreading knowledge about and faith in democracy as a system of government. Authoritarians intending to take over must now contend with a huge mass of support for democracy within their countries, such as they did not face before. Externally, as well, they can less assuredly count on support.

Some other things need to change, however, in order to consolidate these gains. Making democracy more equal in practice for poorer citizens through institutional improvements is an important remaining task. Rather than protecting democracy from poor people, securing democracy *for* them is a more urgent issue.

2

Poor People and Democratic Citizenship in Africa

Michael Bratton

If democracy consists of "rule by the people," then the values, attitudes, and behaviors of ordinary folk are central to considerations of the fate of democracy. If it turns out that democratic stability in the medium- to long-term depends on the economic well-being of citizens, then democracies can be expected to be especially fragile in world regions where many people live in poverty.

This chapter explores the relationship of poor people to democratic citizenship in sub-Saharan Africa. It is prompted in part by intriguing research results emerging from South Asia that suggest that poor people are equally or more likely to hold democratic values, support democratic regimes, and vote in democratic elections. For example, Yadav finds for India in the 1990s "a participatory upsurge" among scheduled castes and tribes leading to "turnout of the lower orders of society...well above that of the most privileged groups" (2000: 120, 133). Bratton, Chu, and Lagos have replicated this result using National Election Survey data for India, confirming that Indians of lower material status were significantly more likely to cast a ballot in the 1999 election (2006).

To test these and related results in African contexts, data are drawn from the Afrobarometer. The Afrobarometer is a series of comparative national surveys that, among other things, measures the economic

This chapter draws upon some materials published previously as an article titled "Populations pauvres et citoyennete democratique en Afrique," in the journal *Afrique Contemporaire*, 220 (4), 33–64, 2006.

living conditions and political orientations of ordinary Africans.[1] Each national survey – covering fifteen countries in Round 2 – is based on a probability sample representing the adult population eighteen years and older. In each round, face-to-face interviews are conducted with more than 21,000 respondents in the language of the respondent's choice. Because the surveys use a standard instrument, comparisons are possible across countries and over time. Although most of the results reported here are from the survey in 2002–2003, occasional comparisons are made with Afrobarometer Round 1 (1999–2001) and Afrobarometer Round 3 (2005–2006).

I start by reviewing the concept and measurement of poverty at the individual level and make a case for the utility of the Afrobarometer's Lived Poverty Index. The second, demographic section provides answers to the query: "Who are the African poor?" and confirms that they tend to be rural and elderly. The chapter then briefly reviews the political values, attitudes, and behaviors of ordinary Africans, concluding that democratic orientations are surprisingly widespread but often shallow. A fourth section analyzes the simple, bivariate effects of lived poverty on various dimensions of democratic citizenship. A fifth section uses multivariate models to test if these results are robust. And a conclusion adds interpretation.

To anticipate results, I find that poor Africans are *no more or less likely* than their wealthier counterparts to hold democratic values or to prefer democracy above other political regimes. But, in recent elections, they vote more frequently than richer people and more regularly attend community meetings between elections. In only two respects, however, is poverty the *main* demographic consideration: poorer people are less likely to judge that African governments are consolidating democracy and more likely to make political contacts with informal political leaders.

---

[1] The Afrobarometer is a network of social scientists in Africa coordinated by the Institute for Democracy in South Africa (Idasa), the Center for Democratic Development (CDD-Ghana), and Michigan State University (MSU). Details on the project's objectives, coverage, questionnaires, sampling, fieldwork, data, and results are available at www.afrobarometer.org.

These results lead to paradoxical conclusions. On the one hand, poor people in Africa are primed to play a role in their own self-governance but are clearly dissatisfied with the quality of rule provided by elected national leaders. On the other hand, they turn out in large numbers for elections but prefer to by-pass the formal channels of the democratic state in attempting to redress political grievances. One interpretation of these results is that the poor majority – especially its older, rural members – remains embedded in informal relations of patron-clientelism. Although poorer people are beginning to attain certain key capabilities of democratic citizenship, they have yet to find ways to make the institutions of democracy work in their favor.

Indicators of Poverty

Poverty is a difficult concept to encapsulate for purposes of research, especially cross-national, comparative research (Atkinson 1987; Clark and Hulme 2005). The first issue is whether poverty is best understood in terms of absolute levels of deprivation or the relative social positions of individuals and groups (Seers 1969; Sen 1976, 1981). Standard metrics of poverty – such as poverty datum lines – do not have universal meaning in all settings. Not only does the purchasing power of any monetary unit vary greatly across countries; the salience of poverty depends critically on surrounding distributions of wealth and opportunity. The same absolute level of poverty will be much more visible in an unequal society and have different social and political consequences than in places where life chances are more evenly distributed.

Second, poverty is a multidimensional concept (Chambers 1983; Sen 1999; Alkire 2002). To be sure, the most basic deprivations are material, such as shortages of land or livestock in agrarian societies, or lack of employment and income in industrial and post-industrial settings. But poverty also has less tangible dimensions such as vulnerability to external shocks, social isolation, and political powerlessness. Poor people lack not only the wherewithal to thrive physically; they also lack the capability to make choices for themselves or, failing that, to obtain help in times of need. A set of purely economic indicators is unlikely to capture the complexity of these manifold dimensions; cross-disciplinary research is required instead (Hulme and Toye 2006).

Third, researchers debate the utility of objective versus subjective indicators of poverty (Narayan et al. 2000; Pradhan and Ravallion 2000; Clark 2002; White 2002). One approach uses concrete criteria to assess the extent of poverty, whether in terms of the proportion of landless people, those living on a dollar a day, or those in the bottom fifth of the income distribution. Although seemingly resting on hard data, this approach does not always generate reliable results or valid inferences to the behavior of poor people. As an antidote, other researchers prefer subjective indicators that record how poor people define poverty or place themselves on a ladder of well-being (e.g., Krishna 2004). The problem with many qualitative definitions and scales is that they are self-anchoring and therefore of limited use for comparative purposes. Moreover, objective and subjective indicators often come up with widely varying estimates of the extent of poverty in any given society (Jodha 1988).

The Afrobarometer contains both objective indicators of absolute poverty and subjective assessments by survey respondents of their relative place in a "poor–rich" hierarchy. Comparisons between indicators therefore becomes possible. The database also allows the construction of an Index of Lived Poverty based on respondent reports of access to a range of basic human needs – that goes a good way toward capturing the complexity of poverty. Based on an individual's recollections of "going without" basic needs, the Index of Lived Poverty is an "experiential" indicator of poverty that mixes objective and subjective approaches (Mattes, Bratton, and Davids 2003). Whether this experiential indicator can help bridge objective–subjective measurement gaps will be tested as the chapter proceeds.

Measuring Poverty in Africa

This section of the chapter describes, compares, and evaluates various competing indicators of poverty as measured by the Afrobarometer at the individual level.

An Objective Indicator: Household Income

In Africa, researchers have found that household income is a poor proxy for poverty. Especially in rural areas, self-provisioning peasants

provide for many of their own basic needs and may have limited interactions with the formal cash economy. If income is produced, it is usually seasonal, depending on the timing of the harvest or the liquidation
of livestock assets to cover periodic or emergency expenses. In urban
areas, where unemployment and underemployment are widespread,
most people piece together livelihoods from a variety of part-time
income streams, whose flow may be intermittent and unpredictable.

As a result, respondents have a hard time calculating correct answers
to survey questions about household income. The Afrobarometer asks:
"Before taxes, how much do you and your spouse together earn
per month?" Quite apart from the challenge of converting seasonal
earnings into monthly increments, the question invites other errors:
some respondents may be unmarried, others may not know what their
spouse earns, and some may live in households with income earners
other than spouses. Add to these concerns the likelihood that some
people will intentionally disguise their true earnings, and it becomes
clear that income data from African surveys must be viewed with considerable skepticism. For this reason, recent rounds of Afrobarometer
surveys have dropped the income question in favor of enumerating
household assets.

Nevertheless, and with due caution, several general features can be
noted about the income data (see Figure 2.1). To begin with, one-
third (34 percent) of respondents report no household income at all.
Moreover, the distribution of income is skewed toward the low-end
of the scale: there are more than three times as many people in the
bottom fifth of the income distribution (29 percent) than in the top
fifth (9 percent). The modal income is in the third decile which, when
averaged across all fifteen countries, is the equivalent of less than
US$2 per day. Taken together, these data confirm a profile across
sub-Saharan countries in which extensive poverty coexists with major
income disparities.

Finally, average measures of income poverty obscure major cross-
national variations (not shown in Figure 2.1). In four countries –
Lesotho, Malawi, Mozambique, and Senegal – over half of the national
sample reports no cash income at all. In three other countries –
Ghana, Mali, and Zambia – about one-half of respondents fall into
the bottom fifth (two deciles) of income earners. Taken together, these

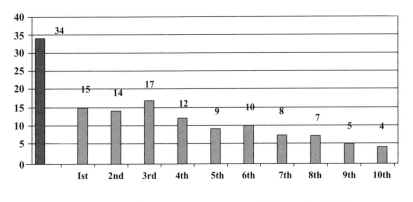

FIGURE 2.1. Distribution of Household Income: Fifteen African Countries, 2002–2003.

seven countries contain the highest proportions of income-poor people among the countries studied in the Afrobarometer.

The Meaning of Poverty

Before searching for alternatives to a standard income indicator, it seems worthwhile to ask how Africans themselves regard poverty. Subjectively, do Africans see poverty as a lack of cash income or in broader, more multidimensional terms?

To this end, the Afrobarometer poses an open-ended question: "In your opinion, what does it mean to be 'poor'?" Respondents are encouraged to offer up to three responses. In 2002–2003, 99 percent could offer at least one definition of poverty, which suggests that the concept is universally understood. Somewhat fewer (81 percent) could offer two definitions but, in offering more than one interpretation, these survey respondents thereby implied that they see poverty in multifaceted terms. Along these lines, a smaller majority (58 percent) could offer three definitions, a capability that was significantly associated with an individual's level of education.

The distribution of popular meanings is displayed in Figure 2.2. The Africans we interviewed most commonly associate being poor with a lack of food, a meaning mentioned by 46 percent of respondents. This

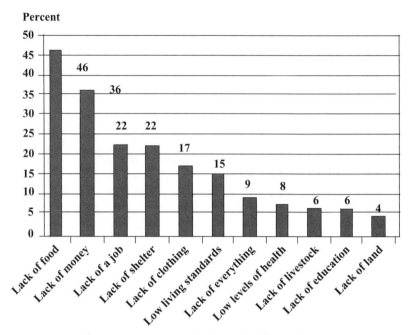

FIGURE 2.2. What Does it Mean to Be "Poor"? Fifteen African Countries, 2002–2003.

connotation draws attention to the fundamental importance of nutritional intake as the basis of economic well-being for many Africans. Interestingly, urban and rural dwellers were about equally likely to see poverty as a lack of food. It seems that, whereas rural dwellers face problems of food insecurity because of the uncertainty of seasonal rainfall, urban dwellers face a parallel problem due to the unpredictability of income flows from part-time or occasional employment. Because an (unknown) proportion of all adults (including some self-described "farmers") purchase at least some food, a subjective perception of poverty as a lack of food is not entirely at odds with an objective definition based on household income.

The connection between poverty and cash income is made explicitly in the second and third most commonly cited meanings of poverty: "lack of money" (mentioned by 36 percent) and "lack of a job" (22 percent). If these responses together amount to two different ways of saying "lack of income," then a majority (58 percent) of Africans interpret poverty in this way. Income-based measures of poverty thus appear to have some conceptual validity, reflecting as they do the increasing monetization of all economic transactions in Africa, including securing daily subsistence.

Other common interpretations of poverty – for example, "lack of shelter," (22 percent) and "lack of clothing" (17 percent) – would also seem to contain an income component, though they also signify social status. Respondents who refer to poverty as "low levels of health" and "lack of education" stretch the concept to embrace a couple of key determinants of life chances. And those who mention shortages of land and livestock emphasize again poverty's material base, but here primarily with reference to fixed assets rather than flows of income.

Contrary to the assumption that Africans possess communal cultures, people rarely interpreted poverty as social isolation: fewer than 4 percent emphasized a "lack of family" or social support network; and an equal proportion preferred to turn the tables by pointing to poverty as an "inability to *meet* family obligations." And less than 1 percent mentioned powerlessness (e.g., "no-one listens to you") or vulnerability (e.g., "having misfortune, bad luck").

All told, however, African conceptions of well-being, although income-based, are qualified by strong connotations of eating adequately and presenting oneself as a well-clothed and well-housed person. There is also recognition that good health and educational attainment offer opportunities for people to obtain social and economic mobility. Oddly underemphasized are the traditional ties of family, kin and community that have often been assumed to protect the individual from lapsing into poverty.

A Subjective Indicator: A Ladder of Well-Being

Using their own definitions, how do Africans locate themselves on a ladder that reaches from poverty to the good life? Specifically, the Afrobarometer asks, "On a scale between 0 and 10, where 0 are 'poor' people and 10 are 'rich' people, which number would you give yourself today?" To help people who were not fully literate or numerate, interviewers were permitted to sketch an eleven-step ladder – with

Percent of Respondents

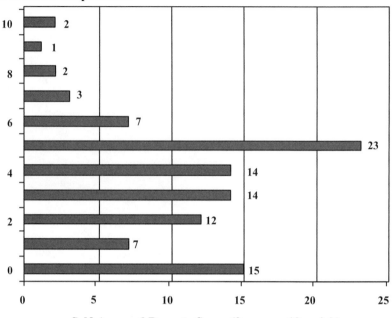

FIGURE 2.3. Ladder of Well-Being.

0 on the bottom rung and 10 on the top rung – on a piece of paper or in the dirt underfoot. With this visual aid, all but 2 percent were able to offer a numeric answer.

The results are displayed on the "ladder" in Figure 2.3. As often happens, people gravitated to the end- and mid-points of the scale. A plurality of respondents (23 percent) located themselves on the middle rung, either because they truly felt they were halfway between poverty and well-being, or because they saw themselves as enjoying an "average" quality of life, or because they were uncertain about how to choose. The next most common response was "poor" as signified by the lowest possible score of 0. And well more than half (62 percent) judged their status to be below the mid-point on the ladder. Only 2 percent saw themselves as rich. On the basis of this evidence, it is hard to avoid the conclusion that, subjectively, most Africans consider themselves to be victims of poverty.

The incidence of self-assessed poverty (mean score = 3.6 on the scale of 0 to 10) varies across and within African countries. Whereas Malawians are most likely to see themselves as poor (mean country score = 1.9), Nigerians and South Africans are the least likely to do so (mean country scores = 4.8 and 4.6 respectively). Note, however, that all mean country scores lie below the middle rung of the ladder.

Poverty perceptions also vary across time. The adult Africans interviewed in 2002–2003 think they are poorer than the previous generation. People place their parents on a significantly higher rung ten years ago (mean score = 4.1) than they place themselves today. A negative generation gap has apparently opened up over the past decade in twelve of the fifteen countries studied and is widest in Senegal (−1.4) and Zambia (−1.5). Only in Botswana (+0.21) and Tanzania (+0.22), do people generally perceive a modest alleviation of poverty during the last ten years.[2]

As for the economic future, Africans are universally optimistic. In every Afrobarometer country, without exception, adults consider that their children will attain greater well-being than themselves (mean score = 6.6). And, by crossing the middle rung, children are expected to climb out of relative poverty. Nigerians are typically exuberant: they expect their children to attain a score of more than 9 on the 10-point scale! Kenyans, Cape Verdeans, Ghanaians, and Batswana also expect their children to be twice as wealthy in the future as they are today. These data provide evidence that, even on a continent where poverty is a daily reality for most people, hope springs eternal.

One wonders, however, about the validity and reliability of a subjective ladder of well-being, especially under conditions where, demonstrably, people define poverty in a variety of ways. To gauge the relative utility of different indicators, I compare the (objective) household income with the (subjective) well-being ladder.[3] Figure 2.4 plots the distribution of both indicators.

---

[2] The poverty situation in Cape Verde reportedly did not change.
[3] To enable comparison, the ladder data are adjusted to match the structure of the income data. The ladder score of 0 is compared directly with "no income." And the percentage shares of ladder score between 1–10 are then recalculated to make them directly comparable with income deciles.

Percent

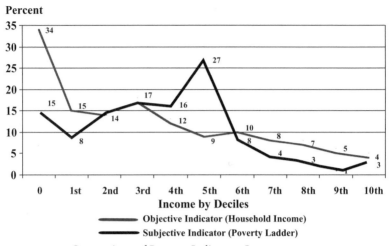

FIGURE 2.4. Comparison of Poverty Indicators I.

I note two major differences and one basic similarity. First, more than twice as many people say they have "no income" as judge themselves to be on the bottom rung of the ladder. This divergence strongly suggests that income is not an essential component of African conceptions of poverty. Stated differently, some people who lack income do not automatically judge themselves to belong among the poorest of the poor. Important in this group would be self-provisioning peasants who cater to their own basic needs largely or wholly outside of the cash economy. Second, three times as many people place themselves on the middle rung of the ladder as in the fifth decile of income-earners. This discrepancy may be due to the proclivity of respondents to locate themselves subjectively in the "middle" when, in objective income terms, the central tendency (mode) is on the third decile. But, again, people may be trying to indicate that, even though they lag behind in earning income, their sense of well-being is on a par with the average citizen. In both these instances, an objective, income-based indicator would classify people as poorer than they subjectively feel themselves to be.

Apart from these major deviations, the two indicators tend to track together, especially in the lower middle and upper ends of each scale. It is striking, for example, that the second and third deciles of income earners place themselves on the second and third rungs of the well-being ladder. And similar slopes connect upper deciles and upper rungs. Thus, there appears to be a degree of overlap between objective and subjective poverty indicators, at least for the one-third of the population that is moderately poor and the one-fifth or more of the population that is relatively rich.

An Experiential Indicator: Index of Lived Poverty

The prior analysis points to the need for an overarching indicator that can capture both objective material resources (notably income) and broader, subjective perceptions of well-being. I have shown that, apart from income deficits alone, Africans define poverty in terms of lack of access to a range of basic human needs. Why not, therefore, ask people to recall their experiences in trying to meet such needs?

The Afrobarometer employs a battery of questions along these lines: "Over the past year, how often, if ever, have you or your family gone without (a) enough food to eat; (b) enough clean water for home use; (c) medicines or medical treatment; (d) electricity in your home; (e) enough fuel to cook your food; and (f) a cash income.[4] Figure 2.5 reports the distribution of people who reported "going without" each necessity at least once during the previous year.

More than half the Africans interviewed reported being able to obtain sufficient fuel for cooking their food and clean water for home use. More than half, however, reported at least occasional shortages of food and medicines. Fully one-fifth reported that access to healthcare was a persistent problem ("many times" or "always"). The limits of electrification, especially rural electrification, in Africa are reflected in the seven out of ten Africans who reported lack of access to electricity; more than half said "many times" or "always," which usually meant that they were entirely unconnected to an electricity grid. The most common experience, however, was with shortfalls of cash income,

---

[4] We adapted and expanded this battery for use in Africa from items first devised by Rose and colleagues for the New Europe Barometer (Rose and Haerpfer 1998, 39–40). Response categories are "never," "just once or twice," "several times," "many times," and "always."

Percent

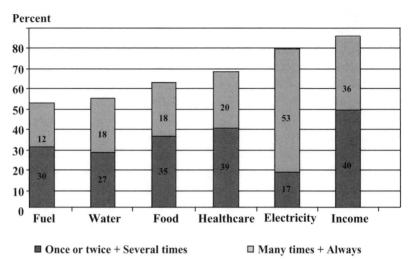

■ **Once or twice + Several times**   □ **Many times + Always**

FIGURE 2.5. Lived Poverty: Percentage Going without Basic Needs.

either intermittent or persistent. Fully three-quarters of all respondents said that they or their families had gone without cash on at least one occasion during the previous year.

Because these existential reports refer to both income flows and other felt needs, they can potentially constitute a hybrid indicator. As it happens, people who experience difficulty in covering one type of basic need usually also have trouble in satisfying all others. Stated differently, all items in the experiential battery hang together into a single, coherent factor, which in turn allowed the construction of a valid and reliable *Index of Lived Poverty*.[5]

As shown in Table 2.1, the Index of Lived Poverty is more highly correlated with both household income and the well-being ladder than either of these indicators is correlated with the other. We take this as evidence that this experiential indicator meets the goal of bridging objective and subjective perspectives on poverty. We expect that this

[5] Factor analysis (maximum likelihood method) extracted a single, reliable factor without rotation: Eigenvalue = 2.628, variance explained = 33 percent, Cronbach's alpha = .723. Electricity was omitted from the Index because of missing values and a low loading on the factor. The index is an average score for all five indicators on the same 5-point scale from "never" to "always."

TABLE 2.1. *Comparison of Poverty Indicators II*

	Household Income	Ladder of Well-Being	Index of Lived Poverty
Household Income	1.000		
Ladder of Well-Being	.204***	1.000	
Index of Lived Poverty[a]	−268***	−.312***	1.000

[a] Because the index measures poverty and the other indicators measure wealth or well-being, relationships are expected to be negative.

*** $p \leq .001$.

item, which combines income with other, less tangible and "in kind" manifestations of well-being (like food, education, and health), is a more valid and reliable construct than either alternative. As a quick guide to levels of poverty, the Lived Poverty battery is also less costly to administer than an in-depth household income and expenditure survey. In sum, as the best single indicator we have discovered to date, I will use the Index of Lived Poverty to measure levels of poverty for the remainder of this chapter.

Who Are the African Poor?

In order to summarize the nature, incidence, and distribution of poverty in sub-Saharan countries, I classify Afrobarometer respondents according to their position on the Index of Lived Poverty (see Table 2.2).

TABLE 2.2. *Classification of African Survey Respondents, by Poverty*

Frequency of Going Without Basic Needs[a]	Response Category	Index Range	Percent Distribution	Classification
Never	0	0	13	Well-to-do
Just Once or Twice	1	0.2 – 1.0	34	Occasionally Poor
Several Times	2	1.2 – 2.0	35	Poor
Many Times	3	2.2 – 3.0	16	Very Poor
Always	4	3.2 – 4.0	2	Destitute

[a] Reference is made to five basic needs: food, clean water, healthcare, cooking fuel, and cash income. The duration of need is the "past year." $N = 17,617$.

At the top of this distribution are those "well-to-do" individuals who, during the year prior to the survey, never went without food, clean water, healthcare, cooking fuel, or cash income. This relatively wealthy elite, which manages to cover its own basic needs, constitutes just 13 percent of all Africans surveyed. They are followed by a group of "occasionally poor" individuals, defined as those who encountered at least one unmet basic need in the last twelve months. Then comes a core population of "poor" people who confronted several shortages of certain basic needs during the same period. The classification is rounded out by "very poor" people (16 percent), who suffer regular and persistent shortages across many basic needs, and by the "destitute" (2 percent), who insist that they "always" lack the essential requirements for a decent life. This rather normal distribution, which places more than two-thirds of the populations surveyed in two middle categories, is consistent with more casual observations about the social distribution of poverty in Africa.

The classification is also validated by the distributions of the various social groups across African countries. As might be expected, the largest proportion of well-to-do people is found in South Africa (40 percent), although Namibia and Ghana are above average in the proportion of the population that reportedly meets basic needs (22 and 18 percent respectively). The largest proportions of self-reported destitute folk are found in Mozambique and Senegal (each 3 percent); and Lesotho and Malawi display the largest proportions of very poor people (33 and 30 percent respectively). The most "typical" African country is Nigeria: the 36 percent of its population who are poor and 34 percent who are occasionally poor represent a microcosm of the subcontinent as a whole.

In the tables that follow, the effects of poverty on democratic citizenship are traced primarily by means of the Index of Lived Poverty, which is an interval scale. But the text provides illustrations by discussing observed differences between particular social groups, whether well-to-do, destitute, or somewhere in between. Occasionally, I even use a shorthand reference to the "non-poor minority" (comprised of the 47 percent in the two wealthiest categories) and the "poor majority" (comprised of the 53 percent in the three poorest categories combined).

Bivariate Correlation Coefficient (r)

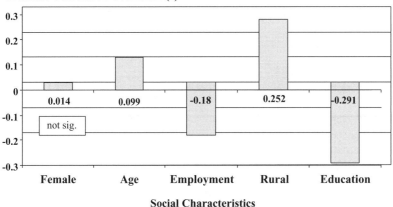

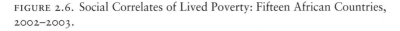

FIGURE 2.6. Social Correlates of Lived Poverty: Fifteen African Countries, 2002–2003.

But who belongs to these strata? Apart from level of poverty, what other social characteristics do their members share? As it happens, *gender* appears to play no meaningful role in distinguishing an individual's poverty status: men and women are equally distributed within each category (see Figure 2.6). This would stand to reason if poverty were a household characteristic rather an individual one, with nuclear family members (notably spouses) having roughly the same socioeconomic status. But the Index apparently fails to capture any differences of well-being within the family arising from gender-based power differentials.

But four other social characteristics, presented in ascending order of importance, show strong and significant connections to the Index of Lived Poverty. First, age correlates positively with poverty. For example, persons sixty or older are ten percentage points more likely than adults thirty or younger to be very poor. Second, naturally enough, poverty is a negative function of employment. The unemployed are twice as likely as those employed full time to be very poor and twice as unlikely to be well-to-do. Third, in Africa, poverty is a predominantly rural phenomenon. To be sure, we find all categories of well-being (or "ill-being") in both cities and countryside. But three times as many members of the poor majority live in rural areas than in urban centers.

Finally and unsurprisingly, poverty and education are inversely related. Indeed, education is the best predictor of an escape from poverty, with a college postgraduate being seven times more likely to be well-to-do than a person with no formal education (42 percent versus 6 percent).

In sum, therefore, the experience of lived poverty in Africa is concentrated among those older, less educated, rural dwellers who also lack formal employment. It is these marginalized and vulnerable people who are most likely to encounter difficulty in fulfilling their basic human needs. The question now arises as to whether this poor majority is also less likely to possess the capabilities of democratic citizenship.

Dimensions of Democratic Citizenship

As a prelude to addressing this question, it is first necessary to parse the concept of democratic citizenship. I distinguish three main dimensions that can be captured using social survey data: *values, attitudes,* and *behaviors.*

Political Values

At root, democratic citizens are distinguished by a set of *value* orientations that underpin popular rule. These values include, inter alia, political tolerance and a desire for political equality and accountability (Inglehart 1997; Gibson and Gouws 2003). Democratic "citizens" – as opposed to autocratic "subjects" (Mamdani 1996) or patrimonial "clients" (Fox 1990) – tolerate a diversity of political opinion, support principles of universal suffrage, and demand that leaders respond to mass needs. The Afrobarometer questionnaire contains survey items that provide insight into these value orientations. Each item offers the respondent two opposing statements, asks them to choose the one closest to their own view, and then probes whether they "agree" or "agree very strongly."

On political *tolerance*, respondents were asked to choose between the following statements: "A. In order to make decisions in our community, we should talk until everyone agrees." or "B. Since we will never agree on everything, we must learn to accept differences of opinion within our community." By this measure, individuals are most tolerant (option B) in Uganda, Kenya, and Namibia (at least 58 percent) and least so in Senegal, Mali, and Mozambique (33 percent or less). Overall, however, the Africans we interviewed were split on this issue, with 50 percent favoring unanimity in public opinion and 46 percent accepting dissent. As such, one can only conclude that the democratic norm of political tolerance has yet to take root in Africa.

Africans seem to speak more clearly about political *accountability*. The survey choice was as follows: "A. As citizens, we should be more active in questioning the actions of our leaders." or "B. In our country these days, there is not enough respect for authority." Fully two-thirds of all respondents (68 percent) said they want to hold leaders accountable (Option A) compared to 27 percent who preferred to defer to authority. This time, Ugandans, Ghanaians, and Malawians led the way (at 80 percent or more) with only Namibians seeing virtue in respectfully submitting (58 percent chose Option B). Apart from this single exception, and perhaps because of hard-won experience with bad governance, Africans otherwise seem to consider that the power of incumbent rulers must be checked.

Finally, the survey item on political *equality* posed a contrast between "A. All people should be permitted to vote, even if they do not understand all the issues in an election." and "B. Only those who are sufficiently well educated should be allowed to choose our leaders." In this instance the citizenship value was clearly ascendant. Many more Africans favored universal suffrage (78 percent) than a qualified franchise (17 percent). This principle was pervasive in Kenya, Senegal, and Cape Verde (85 percent or higher) and was valued by a two-thirds majority in all countries except Mozambique and South Africa. If nothing else (and other values remain contested), Africans have embraced political equality, a core value of democratic citizenship.

Political Attitudes

Beyond fundamental values, citizenship in a democracy involves a distinctive set of mass political attitudes. Among other things, citizens are expected to be committed to democracy as a preferred political regime and to express satisfaction with its supply. Unlike political values, which are imbibed in childhood and are slow to change, political attitudes may be learned in adulthood, often quickly and even fleetingly, on the basis of direct firsthand experiences with different political regimes.

The Afrobarometer measures the standard set of political attitudes usually found in barometer-type surveys worldwide, plus several original items. As reported elsewhere, the sum total of these measurements reveals an African populace with favorable attitudes to democracy that are widespread but shallow (Bratton, Mattes and Gyimah-Boadi 2005).

On the demand side, most Africans – some 64 percent in 2002–2003 – say that they "*prefer democracy* to any other kind of government." But this average "continental" score masks cross-country variations over time, with low support for democracy gradually rising in Lesotho, but with initially high support quickly falling in Nigeria. At the same time, the Africans we interviewed clearly *reject the ancient régimes* of military, one-party and one-person rule that prevailed on the continent from independence to the 1990s. For example, three-quarters consistently abjure the notions that "the army comes in to govern the country" or that "elections and parliament are abolished so that the president can decide everything."

What is much less certain, however, is the depth of these commitments. Some people do little more than pay lip service to democracy because support for this regime coexists with a willingness to simultaneously countenance one or more autocratic alternatives. Indeed, in 1999–2001, fewer than half of all respondents (48 percent) *both* supported democracy *and* rejected all three authoritarian regimes. And this index of demand for democracy fell to just over one in three respondents (37 percent) by 2002–2003 (Bratton 2004).

On the supply side, popular *satisfaction with "the way democracy works"* has also settled at a relatively low level, with some 54 percent satisfied across fifteen African countries in 2002–2003. And the same proportion felt that that their country was either "a full democracy" or a "democracy with (only) minor problems." Both these averages, however, conceal considerable variation across countries and volatility over time. Although satisfaction with democracy has steadily risen in Ghana, it has plummeted in Nigeria. And whereas Malians have come to believe that problems with their new democracy are minor only,

Malawians have lost faith that democracy can solve their country's deep-seated problems of development and governance.

Beyond these standard items, the Afrobarometer probes several original attitudes to democracy. The first concerns *support for democratic institutions* on the assumption that elections, parties, the legislature, and the presidency are more tangible referents for survey respondents than the abstract concept of "democracy." We find that Africans overwhelmingly (79 percent) prefer to "choose leaders in this country through regular, open, and honest elections" than by any other means (Afrobarometer Network 2004). Given past experiences with leaders who overstayed their welcome, the electorate also favors term limits on the presidency (74 percent). Concomitantly, they prefer that the parliament make laws for the country, "even if the president does not agree" (61 percent). People are somewhat more cautious and divided, however, about political parties: whereas a slim majority acknowledges that, "many political parties are needed... for real choices" (55 percent), a sizeable minority fears that "political parties create division and confusion" (40 percent).[6] And, as with political values, isolated expressions of support for various separate institutions have yet to cohere into a single, overall factor of support for democratic institutions generally.

Second, we measure *political patience*. Respondents are asked to choose whether "A. Our present system of elected government should be given more time to deal with inherited problems." or "B. If our present system cannot produce results soon, then we should try another form of government." Reassuringly, Africans are not eager to abandon democracy: By a twenty-point margin (56 percent versus 36 percent in 2002–2003), they choose to stick with their present system of elected government rather than to cast it aside. But, this patience is not inexhaustible. For the five countries where we have comparable data, the level of political patience dropped from 73 percent to 63 percent over the three-year interval between the first two surveys.

---

[6] Especially in Uganda, Senegal, and Lesotho, where majorities associate parties with conflict.

Finally, we sought to measure the nature of popular support for democracy. Is it *intrinsic*, based on the inherent qualities of democracy itself, such as civil liberties and political rights? Or is support *instrumental*, being granted only conditionally – for example, if democracy improves economic standards of living or the delivery of social services? The question took the familiar forced choice format: Agree with A or B? "A. Democracy is worth having simply because it allows everyone a free and equal voice in making decisions." or "B. Democracy is only worth having if it can address everyone's basic social and economic needs." Somewhat to our surprise, and contrary to expectations in much of the literature (Ake 1996; but see Bratton and Mattes 2001a, 2001b), we found more intrinsic (50 percent) than instrumental (38 percent) support for democracy. One out of ten people "didn't know." This result gives reason to counter the conventional wisdom that democracy will automatically founder in Africa because governments fail to deliver socioeconomic development.

Political Behavior

Democracy also requires active citizens. Not only are individuals in a democracy obliged to exercise their right to vote, but they are also expected, between elections, to engage with others in collective action and to take initiatives to contact their leaders.

According to the Afrobarometer, Africans participate in the political process at quite high levels. Take *voting*. To be sure, Africans were somewhat less likely to turn out for recent presidential and parliamentary elections (70 percent) than were East Asians (74 percent) and Latin Americans (76 percent; Bratton, Chu and Lagos 2006). But low voter turnout rates in places like Zimbabwe (44 percent in 1996) are offset by high turnout rates in places like Ghana (89 percent in 1996[7]). And, generally speaking, Africans tend to appear at the polls more frequently than the citizens of certain advanced democracies, notably the United States and Switzerland.

As for *collective action*, Africans are slightly more likely than East Asians to regularly discuss politics with others (20 percent versus 18

---

[7] Self-reported turnout rate of eligible voters from Afrobarometer Round 1.

percent[8]), but less likely to do so than Latin Americans (31 percent). Africans nevertheless evince high levels of voluntary association – for example, a majority (52 percent) claims to be an active member or official leader in a religious group like a church, sect, or mosque. Africans are also distinguished by regular attendance at community meetings (47 percent say they did this "several times" or "often" during the previous year) and by informally "joining with others to raise an issue" (33 percent). They even report comparatively high levels of unconventional political participation, with 14 percent saying they joined a demonstration or a protest march.

But parochial patterns are evident in popular *contacts with leaders*. Ordinary Africans are twice as likely to contact an elected local government councilor (25 percent had done this within the previous year) than their representative to the national legislature (12 percent) or an official of a national government ministry (13 percent). These results suggest that the central state remains a relatively remote and inaccessible apparatus to most Africans. Instead, ordinary people who want to accomplish a personal or collective goal are more likely to use familiar channels to religious leaders (45 percent had done this within the previous year), traditional rulers (32 percent, mostly rural folk), or "some other influential person" (26 percent). Thus, we find a strong predilection among Africans to bypass the official state in favor of informal relations with notables in the local community. This preference is a product both of the physical remoteness of public officials from many (especially rural) citizens but also of the vast social and status distances that exist between the poor or illiterate and the wielders of political power.

Poverty and Democratic Citizenship

Having outlined the broad distributions of democratic values, attitudes, and behaviors among Africans, we are now well placed to inquire whether these attributes vary according to an individual's experience of living in poverty. As discussed earlier, I will use the Afrobarometer's Index of Lived Poverty as the operational predictor.

---

[8] Due to a large sample size – almost 52,000 cases across three continents – this small difference is statistically significant.

TABLE 2.3. *The Effects of Poverty on Democratic Values*

		Dependent Variable	Point Spread[a]	Bivariate Correlation (Pearson's r)[b]
Poor are	Less likely	To be politically tolerant	−7	−.040***
	Equally likely	To want political accountability	+2	not sig.
	More likely	To want political equality	+12	+.051***

[a] Represents widest spread between categories on 5-point poverty scale, usually between destitute and well-to-do people. Cell n's for destitute may be small. Exceptional categories are noted in the text.

[b] Based on 5-point poverty scale from destitute to well-to-do (***$p \leq .001$). Question wordings for dependent variables are given in the text.

As a rough guide, one can hypothesize that the poorer the person, the less likely that he or she will display the capabilities of democratic citizenship. As we shall see, this generic hypothesis is borne out in some respects, but with many exceptions of theoretical and substantive importance.

Poverty and Democratic Values

The differential effects of poverty on democratic citizenship are immediately evident with respect to political values. As expected, poorer people are less politically tolerant than are wealthier people; nonetheless, they are more likely to favor political equality. The results that support these crosscutting conclusions are shown in Table 2.3.

On political *tolerance*, we find that destitute people are 7 percentage points *less* likely than well-to-do people to strongly agree that, "we must learn to accept differences of opinion within our community." Instead, poorer folk are significantly more likely to favor a consensual approach to decision making in which groups of people "talk until they agree" on unanimous, collective points of view. Social unity and political consensus are obviously valuable commodities in societies where political differences can easily escalate, at either community or national levels, into conflict and violence. And one can even plausibly argue that, as a political procedure, consensus building is no less democratic than open competition. But it is difficult to make a case that the absence of difference, pluralism, and minority opinion is consistent with democracy. As such, poorer Africans seem less willing to risk attachment to political tolerance, a core democratic value, than Africans whose well-being is more secure.

By contrast, disadvantaged Africans are much *more* committed than their well-to-do compatriots to the democratic value of political *equality*. By a margin of twelve percentage points, the very poor consider that "all people should be permitted to vote, even if they do not understand all the issues in an election." To be sure, there is a good deal of self-interest embedded in this value because poor people stand to benefit if decisions are made on the basis of the crude political arithmetic of majority rule. But there is also no gainsaying the fact that the poor do profess a belief in the principle of universal adult suffrage, a cornerstone of modern democratic theory. It is mainly wealthier people who express doubts about the wisdom of majority rule. The rich distrust the passions of a mass electorate, perhaps because they fear that these may be turned against property and privilege. As a result, the non-poor minority tends to align itself with the anti-democratic sentiment that "only those who are sufficiently well educated should be allowed to choose our leaders."

Between these diverse effects, we discover that poverty does not shape values of political *accountability*. The small gap in preferences for leadership accountability between the destitute and the well-to-do is not statistically significant. Indeed, *identical* proportions of the poor majority and the non-poor minority (68 percent each) express the norm that "we should be more active in questioning the actions of our leaders." Stated differently, about two out of three African adults, regardless of social stratum, have apparently arrived at a common understanding that it is better to actively check, rather than blindly respect, political leaders.

Thus, the effects of poverty on popular attachments to core democratic values are decidedly mixed. Although poverty suppresses political tolerance, it amplifies commitments to political equality. And poverty has no discernible effect on a widespread popular demand for political accountability. This combination of values suggests that poor people in Africa will not easily surrender their voting rights and may sometimes even use these rights to discipline poorly performing leaders. At the same time, they may too easily acquiesce en bloc to leaders who claim a popular mandate, but who ride roughshod over the rights of dissenting minorities.

Poverty and Democratic Attitudes

The effects of poverty on political attitudes are much more consistent. Moreover, the effects are *always negative*, at least for the range of democratic attitudes we have measured. Without exception, higher levels of lived poverty are associated with lower levels of both demand for democracy and satisfaction with democracy's supply. As such, the Afrobarometer results are consistent with Shin's observation that, in South Korea, "it is low-income people, not the wealthiest, who are least committed to regime change and future democratic reforms" (1999, 83).

Let us start on the demand side. Destitute people are fourteen percentage points less likely than well-to-do people to consider that "democracy is always preferable." And, they are consistently less likely to reject all authoritarian alternatives, such as one-person rule (minus eleven points), one-party rule (minus twelve points), and military rule (minus thirteen points). Reflecting the fact that poverty in Africa is most prevalent among elderly rural dwellers, the poor are least likely to reject a traditional form of government led by chiefs, headmen, or councils of elders (minus nineteen points). This nostalgia for the past apart, poverty is most strongly connected to democratic citizenship in terms of an index of demand for democracy. The poor majority is significantly less likely than the non-poor minority to display deep commitments to democracy. That is, poor Africans do not simultaneously prefer this regime *and* reject *all* previous forms of dictatorship.

Poverty also suppresses popular perceptions that democracy is being supplied. Now by seventeen percentage points, destitute people are less likely than well-to-do people to express satisfaction with the day-to-day performance of elected democratic regimes. And by an even wider margin (nineteen points), the destitute are less inclined than the well-to-do to think that a full, or close to full, democracy is being consolidated

TABLE 2.4. *The Effects of Poverty on Democratic Attitudes*

		Dependent Variable	Point Spread[a]	Bivariate Correlation (Pearson's r)[b]
Poor are	Less likely	To prefer democracy	−14	−.068***
	Less likely	To reject authoritarian alternatives	−11 to −19	−.045***
Thus,	Less likely	To demand democracy	(index)	−.073***
	Less likely	Be satisfied with way democracy works	−17	−.054***
	Less likely	To perceive extensive democracy	−19	−.074***
Thus,	Less likely	To perceive a supply of democracy	(construct)	−.073***
	Less likely	To value democracy intrinsically	−14	−.050***
	Less likely	To support key democratic institutions	−10	−.051***
	Less likely	To be patient with democracy	−13	−.054***

[a] Represents widest spread between categories on 5-point poverty scale, usually between destitute and well-to-do people. Cell n's for destitute may be small. Exceptional categories are noted in the text.

[b] Based on 5-point poverty scale from destitute to well-to-do (***$p \leq .001$). Question wordings for dependent variables are given in the text.

in their country. As expected, lived poverty is strongly and negatively associated with an average construct comprised of these two intertwined indicators, which we summarize as the supply of democracy.

Possible reasons for poverty's negative effects on democratic attitudes are indicated at the bottom of Table 2.4. First, poverty decreases the tendency that an individual will view democracy intrinsically (as an end in itself) and increases the prospect that she will see it instrumentally (as a means to another, often material, end). I suspect that poor people are more prone than others to lose faith in democracy if elected governments fail to meet mass expectations for improved living standards. Second, poor people display lower levels of support for a full battery of key democratic institutions – including open elections, multiple parties, legislative sovereignty, and presidential term limits. I would venture that poor people who do not fully appreciate the concept of divided government find it difficult to accurately assess the essential contributions of these counterbalancing institutions. Finally, as a consequence, poor people are less likely to be patient (minus thirteen points) with the slow, messy, and imperfect processes of decision making in a real-world democracy.

Poverty and Democratic Behaviors

Compared with attitudes to democracy, poverty's relationship to mass action is somewhat less consistent. But the linkage is markedly more *positive*. In important respects, poverty in Africa is associated with *higher levels of political participation*.

The most remarkable result concerns *voting*. Across twelve African countries in Afrobarometer Round 1 (circa 2000), members of the poor majority were somewhat and significantly *more* likely than the non-poor elite to report having voted in the last national election.[9] The same pattern holds even more strongly for Afrobarometer Round 3 (circa 2005), at least for the six countries for which data were available at the time of writing. In 2000, the very poor were four percentage points more likely to vote than the well-to-do; in 2005, they were nine points more likely to do so. Except for Namibia in Round 1, the pattern of higher turnout among the poor majority held in *every* country over *both* time periods. And on both occasions, the gap between destitute and well-to-do people was widest in Botswana, rising from thirteen points in 1999 to twenty-one points in 2005. Because many of Botswana's economically secure citizens apparently abstain from electoral politics, this result tends to undercut the country's reputation as a model African democracy.

The African evidence runs counter to the conventional wisdom about voter turnout in advanced industrial democracies. The literature on the latter regimes indicates that low socioeconomic status usually

---

[9] This result goes beyond the finding of no difference in voter turnout for Africa reported in Bratton, Chu, and Lagos (2006). This chapter used a cruder, binary measure of poverty based on whether respondents had "ever" or "never" experienced shortages of just three basic needs.

depresses political participation (Almond and Verba 1965; Rosenstone and Hansen 1993; Verba, Nie, and Kim 1978; Verba, Schlozman, and Brady 1995). For example, Teixeira (1992) notes an income-based class gap in turnout in the United States that gradually widened over three previous decades. The clear implication is that poverty and voting combine differently in new versus old democracies.

Poverty's influences are murkier for *collective action* between elections. On the one hand, the poor are less likely than the wealthy to engage in political discussions during the regular course of daily life. On the other hand, the poor – especially the very poor – are significantly predisposed to attend community meetings. This last finding can be taken as an encouraging sign of mass involvement in politics beyond the act of voting. But, when paired with limited political discussion, it could also reveal low quality participation. My working hypothesis is that participation by poor people is rarely *autonomous*, meaning that it does not reflect strong individual attachments to personal values and attitudes that have been tested in political debate. On the contrary, I expect poor people's participation to be more *mobilized*, or a product of a process of groupthink that is mass-produced in collective settings such as community meetings.

Poverty also has mixed effects on *contacts between leaders and constituents*. As expected, poor people hold back from approaching government officials, perhaps because the state has no local presence or because they feel a lack of social or economic standing. Nevertheless, poor people do liaise easily with local government councilors; these elected representatives share a similar social status and live in the locality. Thus, there is trace evidence (see contrasting signs on the coefficients in Table 2.5) that central government in African countries may be captured by wealthier elites and that local government is the preserve principally of the poor.

The most striking result concerns contacts with *informal leaders*. In the strongest relationship discovered so far, destitute people are twenty-five percentage points more likely than well-to-do people to direct political demands along informal channels. In order of importance, the poor majority chooses to approach traditional authorities, religious leaders, and other local notables (like businesspeople) when they require a solution to a problem. The popular political choice

TABLE 2.5. *The Effects of Poverty on Democratic Behaviors*

		Dependent Variable	Point Spread[a]	Bivariate Correlation (Pearson's *r*)[b]
Poor are	More likely	To vote (circa 2000)	+4	+.036***
		To vote (circa 2005)	+9	+.069***
	Less likely	To discuss politics	−3	−.025***
	More likely	To attend a community meeting	+10	+.111***
	Less likely	To attend a protest demonstration	−6	−.034***
	Less likely	To contact a government official	−4	−.021***
	More likely	To contact a local govt. councilor	+11	+.068***
	More likely	To contact an informal leader[c]	+25	+.161***

[a] Represents widest spread between categories on 5-point poverty scale, usually between destitute and well-to-do people. Cell n's for destitute may be small. Exceptional categories are noted in the text.

[b] Based on 5-point poverty scale from destitute to well-to-do (***$p \leq .001$). Question wordings for dependent variables are given in the text.

[c] An index, distinguished by factor analysis, of contacts with religious leaders, traditional authorities, and "other influential persons" (Alpha = .617).

of informal patron–client ties over formal channels reflects the twin facts that central government is remote and local government is under-resourced. As such, poor people may be doubly marginalized: they cannot reach the parts of the state where resources reside; and the local authorities that fall within their ambit are themselves notoriously poor and weak.

Interrogating Poverty's Political Effects

So far, we have only considered poverty's simple (bivariate) connections to democratic citizenship. But do these coarse effects survive when poverty is controlled for other demographic factors? I have previously described the social identities of the African poor (see Figure 2.6). Now I argue that it is reasonable to expect that age, residential location, education, and employment status may independently shape individual attachments to democracy. Thus, in this final section, I use multivariate analysis to test whether poverty's political effects are robust to these alternative social influences.

If the effects of poverty are spurious, opposite, or secondary, then telltale signs will appear. First, we already know that several bivariate relationships between poverty and democratic citizenship are quite weak. Thus, poverty's putative effects may turn out to be due to other social considerations. The key signal would be a loss of statistical significance on the lived poverty variable in multivariate models. Second, a change of signs on coefficients of association that is due to the introduction of statistical controls would suggest that we had initially assumed the wrong direction to any poverty effect. Finally, the explanatory rank order of predictors must be examined wherever poverty is one of several independent social factors that are significantly related to democratic citizenship. Unless standardized regression coefficients confirm that poverty is the strongest demographic predictor, we must conclude that its influence is merely secondary.

I find that many of poverty's political effects are indeed conditional on other aspects of social structure. Out of eight select aspects of democratic citizenship,[10] the poverty relationship is spurious for four, including for *every* political value (see Tables 2.6A and 2.6B). The poverty connection is moderate, but secondary, on two additional aspects of citizenship. Importantly, however, *poverty survives all tests* in explaining popular perceptions of the extent of democracy (a political attitude) and contacts with informal political leaders (a political behavior). For these critical dimensions of citizenship, an individual's experience with lived poverty is the *principal* social determinant.

Democratic Values (Controlled)

Take *democratic values* first. Once controlled for other social factors, poverty loses statistical significance on both political tolerance and political equality (see first two columns of figures in Table 2.6A).

Instead, *tolerance* is primarily a function of an individual's access to education. This clear result suggests that education of any kind (not

---

[10] In the interest of brevity, I chose to examine only the aspects of democratic citizenship with which poverty had a strong bivariate relationship.

TABLE 2.6A. *The Conditional Effects of Poverty on Democratic Citizenship, with Controls for Other Demographic Factors (Part I)*

	Democratic Values		Democratic Attitudes	
	Political Tolerance	Political Equality	Demand for Democracy	Supply of Democracy
Lived Poverty	.007	.008	−.011	−.119***
Gender (Female)	.008	.006	−.076***	−.019*
Age	.022*	.007	.027***	.002
Employed	.035***	−.024**	−.013	−.005
Rural	−.001	.064***	.006	.086***
Education	.156***	−.062***	.205***	−.079***

Note: Cell entries are standardized OLS regression coefficients (beta).
Bold figures in shaded cells signify robust poverty effect.
*** $p \leq .001$, ** $p \leq .01$, * $p \leq .05$.

just civic education) widens people's horizons, exposes them to new viewpoints, and enhances values conducive to democracy (Nie, Junn, and Stehlik-Barry 1996; Sullivan and Transue 1999). Even primary schooling under autocratic regimes in Africa seems to have this positive effect (Evans and Rose, forthcoming). Of course, other social processes

TABLE 2.6B. *The Conditional Effects of Poverty on Democratic Citizenship, with Controls for Other Demographic Factors (Part II)*

	Democratic Behaviors			
	Vote 1999–2001	Vote 2005	Attend Community Meeting	Contact Informal Leader
Lived Poverty	.047 (.012)	.128*** (.052)	.109***	.158***
Gender (Female)	−.039	.031	−.087***	−.069***
Age	.037*** (.200)	.047*** (.247)	.079***	.100***
Employed	.070* (.026)	.390*** (.147)	.024**	−.010
Rural	.258*** (.056)	.230*** (.045)	.185***	.141***
Education	−.003	−.058*** (−.042)	.101***	.121***

Note: Cell entries in normal font are standardized OLS regression coefficients.
Italicized entries are unstandardized logistic regression coefficients.
Bold figures in shaded cells signify robust poverty effect.
*** $p \leq .001$, ** $p \leq .01$, * $p \leq .05$.

are positive for tolerance too, such as the natural cycle of aging (older Africans are more tolerant than the young) and the experience of holding a paid job (perhaps because employment leads to interaction with workmates from diverse backgrounds who may hold competing ideas).

Education and employment also affect a person's commitments to political *equality*, but this time in a negative direction. These results are consistent with the earlier observation that wealth undermines egalitarian values. Only now, education and employment displace wealth (and thus poverty) as a meaningful predictor. Just as important as education is residential location: living in a rural area is positive and significant for valuing political equality. My amended interpretation is as follows: although poor people in rural areas value political equality, they do so because of some attribute of residential location and not essentially because they are poor. Perhaps communal cultural norms play a role in promoting egalitarianism among country dwellers, but examination of this prospect must await a future study.[11]

Democratic Attitudes (Controlled)

As for *democratic attitudes*, it turns out that, other things being equal, poverty remains a significant factor only on the supply side. As far as demand for democracy is concerned, other social considerations matter more (see last two columns in Table 2.6A).

Demand for democracy is again driven by education. As people accumulate years of schooling, they become ever more likely to say they prefer democracy and (especially) to reject various authoritarian alternatives. Individuals with some primary schooling may pay lip service to democracy, but they do not understand this concept well and continue to harbor nostalgia for strongman rule. By the time they reach postsecondary level, however, educated people come out clearly, not only *for* democracy, but also *against* autocracy, particularly *contra* military and one-person rule. This sequence of attitude formation via schooling (pro-democracy first, anti-autocracy later), plus the cumulative effects of media exposure and voluntary association, suggest that

---

[11] An individual's support for the value of political equality is related to a willingness to put collective above individual interests, though not strongly ($r = .033^{***}$).

the acquisition of deep democratic commitments is a cognitive learning process (Bratton et al., 2005).

It is also notable that, although women are no poorer or richer than men, they are significantly less likely to demand democracy. Apparently, there is a sizeable gender gap in the political regime preferences of men and women that is not accounted for by (nonexistent) differentials in poverty or even by (sizeable) differences in educational attainment (Logan and Bratton 2006).

As stated earlier, poverty's effects on democratic attitudes are evident only on the *supply side*. Even after an array of alternative social influences is included, an individual's experience with lived poverty clearly undermines his or her assessment of whether the elected government of the day is actually building a consolidated democracy. To be sure, education is also important in inducing people to adopt skeptical attitudes toward democratic performance. By contrast, living in a rural area apparently dulls critical faculties; country dwellers are somewhat more prone to accept any type of political regime that governing elites choose to deliver.

But, other things being equal, *poverty is the single most important social factor shaping popular assessments about the quality of African democracies*. This finding is robust to all the tests we have devised here. And, given that poor people tend to view democracy instrumentally, I infer that unfulfilled popular expectations of improved well-being lead people to conclude that the quality of democracy is therefore low. At the same time, most Africans, including poor Africans still prefer democracy to all other plausible or known regime alternatives. Despite disappointments with the quality of African democracies in practice, the poor in Africa clearly do not constitute an anti-democratic constituency.

Democratic Behaviors (Controlled)

Finally, let us account for *democratic behaviors* (see Table 2.6B). With reference to elections prior to 2001, the finding that *poor people vote more frequently* at first seems to disappear (compare Table 2.6B with Table 2.5). Poverty is displaced by age (with older folk voting more frequently than youngsters) and by residential location (with rural dwellers turning out more often than their urban cousins). Moreover, the same analysis conducted with 2005 data confirms the importance of rival social influences: age and employment lead the way and rurality is still influential.

But, in 2005, and despite controls, *poverty survives* as one of several formative influences on voting in Africa's most recent round of elections. As before, the relationship remains positive, with destitute people being 13 percent more likely than well-to-do people to cast a ballot. Although we will continue to monitor this relationship in subsequent Afrobarometer surveys, I see no reason at this stage to amend the claim that, in Africa, *poor people are more reliable voters than rich people*.

But further discussion is required of the changing results for voting between 2000 and 2005. We know that urban uprisings, including the political mobilization of the urban poor, helped to prompt political liberalization and democratic transitions in Africa in the early 1990s (Bratton and van de Walle 1997). By the end of the decade, however, the urban poor appear to have become demobilized. The weak association between poverty and voting in 1999–2001 signifies this state of affairs, even as voting was vigorous in rural areas – where most poor people live. Since that time, the urban poor must have become *remobilized* because, despite a control for residential location, *poverty* becomes statistically significant in 2005. I surmise that the urban poor relaxed politically after democratic transitions, thinking that regime change would meet their aspirations. When it did not (and this became apparent by 2005), the urban poor rejoined the rural poor in turning out for elections in relatively large numbers.

To conclude empirical analysis, we revisit *political participation between elections*. The introduction of multiple social controls *does not displace poverty* as an influential catalyst of attendance at community meetings or informal contacts with political leaders. Indeed, an individual's experience with lived poverty remains a strong and significant predictor of both these forms of participation (see Table 2.6B), a result that holds true even when country fixed effects are taken into account.

A full range of social factors, all of which are statistically significant, help to explain who *attends community meetings*. Only rural residence does a better job than lived poverty in predicting attendance. The results indicate that the rural poor are the backbone of organized collective action in African countries. Whether the rural poor assemble

in community meetings at their own initiative or at the behest of agencies of mobilization is not, however, altogether obvious from these
data. Nor is it clear whether such meetings provide venues for ordinary
people to articulate demands upward into the political system or for
political elites – both national and local – to discipline and control a
far-flung electorate.

I lean toward the latter interpretation because, when left to their
own devices, ordinary Africans prefer to avoid the apparatus of the
state and to pursue politics through informal channels. Indeed, *the
largest and clearest poverty effects in this study concern contacts with
informal political leaders*. In the last column of Table 2.6B, an individual's experience with lived poverty is a strong, positive predictor
that he or she will seek assistance from a traditional, religious, or other
influential leader. We found earlier that poverty had its largest bivariate effects on informal contacts. We can now confirm that, notwithstanding a full array of controls (which show that rural dwellers and
educated people also resort to informal political contacts), *poverty
supersedes alternative explanations of who contacts informal leaders*.

Conclusions and Interpretations

This chapter set out to examine whether poor people in Africa display
some of the basic capabilities of democratic citizenship. It concludes
that, although mass publics have begun to transform themselves from
clients to citizens, they are embarked on a long-term process that is
far from complete. Moreover, although poverty sometimes facilitates
citizenship, it often remains an obstacle yet to be overcome.

In an effort to capture the elusive concept of poverty, I argued that
the Afrobarometer's Index of Lived Poverty spans diverse approaches
to measurement. As a summary indicator of an individual's access
to basic human needs, the Index contains an income component but
also addresses broader dimensions of poverty. Moreover, the empirical
distribution of the Index confirms that poverty is both widespread and
a disproportionately rural phenomenon in Africa.

Holding other social factors constant, this chapter reports three
general findings about democratic citizenship.

First, poverty is *neutral* for attachments to democratic values: other
things being equal, people at all levels of material well-being tend to

have similar views on political tolerance, political accountability, and political equality. In this regard, there is no reason to believe that the poor are any less attached than any other Africans to basic notions of self-rule.

Second, poverty is *negative* for attitudinal commitments to democracy. On the supply side, poorer people are less inclined than wealthier people to think they are *getting* democracy from current African governments. But, on the demand side, we cannot be certain if poor people actually *want* less of this political regime.[12] In other words, we cannot reject the claim that poor people are no less likely than anyone else to have "faith in democracy." To be sure, this endorsement of democracy's universal appeal is lukewarm at best. But it does signal the clear absence of an anti-democratic constituency among the African poor.

Third, and perhaps surprisingly, poverty is actually *positive* for several important aspects of political participation. The African evidence supports Yadav's (2000) contention that voter turnout is more frequent among poor people, at least for elections in six African countries since turn of the century. Most important, poverty is also positive for popular political activity *between* elections, especially in terms of a person's attendance at community meetings and contacts with informal leaders. These political acts are probably more meaningful to ordinary folk than occasional balloting in intermittent national elections. If so, then popular engagement in local political life on a day-to-day basis should be highly conducive to democracy building.

But is it? Much depends on the quality of collective action and the nature of leadership contacts. Let us remember that the poor, as well as being rural, are predominantly older residents with limited access to formal education and paid employment. Further research is required to determine whether these people attend community meetings at their own initiative and with the intent of lobbying on behalf of their own interests. An uncharitable, but probably realistic interpretation would have national and local elites mobilizing the elderly rural poor to passively assemble to receive instructions, including for whom to vote. My own view is that, whereas mobilized voting seems to be widespread, it cannot represent a permanent state of affairs;

---

[12] The relationship on demand for democracy, although negative, is not statistically significant.

political clients are unlikely to remain loyal indefinitely to patrons who fail to reliably provide material benefits. Instead they will learn how to demand the political accountability they clearly say they want. Further research is also required on whether poor people approach traditional, religious, and other informal leaders as advocates or supplicants. Are their approaches to leaders couched in the dependent idiom of patron–clientelism or as the independent rights-driven demands of free citizens? The data reviewed here suggest that, although clientelism remains alive and well, there are strong new strands of citizenship among the attitudes of the African poor. As such, this large and previously marginalized segment of African societies appears to have embarked on a long, gradual, and uneven transition from clientelism to citizenship.

3

Do Poor People Care Less for Democracy?

Testing Individual-Level Assumptions with Individual-Level Data from India

Anirudh Krishna

The positive effect of higher wealth on democracy was asserted by Lipset (1960: 31): "democracy is related to the state of economic development . . . the more well-to-do a nation, the greater the chances it will sustain democracy." Later studies have overwhelmingly reaffirmed this association between wealth and democracy. However, why the association should hold remains unexplained in terms of microfoundations. The causal mechanisms linking development to democracy "remain, in effect, a black box" (Rueschmeyer, Stephens, and Stephens 1992: 29); "there is little agreement as to why high income per capita . . . virtually guarantees that democracy will remain in place" (Bunce 2000: 707); the literature "suffers from ambiguities of its own" (Przeworski and Limongi 1993: 62); and it has "generated a long series of complex, competing, and largely untested hypotheses" (Remmer 1995: 107).

Alternative hypotheses were reviewed in the introductory chapter, suggesting that the missing causal mechanism is to be found in richer individuals' greater concern for democracy. As incomes grow, it is proposed, people tend to have more interest in and greater support for democracy. Three variants of this hypothesis have been put forward, although none has been tested empirically at the individual level.

A hierarchy-of-needs hypothesis provides the first clue as to why poor people might care less for democracy. A second clue was provided by hypotheses proposing value shifts and changes in culture. As people become richer, they are expected in this hypothesis, to acquire more of the values associated with respect for freedom and civil and political liberties. These effects of higher wealth might be experienced with some time lag. On the whole, richer individuals should show more support for democracy. The first and second hypotheses come together in the expectation that a growing middle class will serve as a driving force for democracy. A third hypothesis proposes inequality as an intervening variable between economic development and preference for democracy. Individual preferences for democracy, especially those of richer individuals, are inversely related to the extent of income inequality, it is proposed, because richer individuals fear that democracy in more unequal societies might go together with progressive taxation. Because economic development has been associated, in general, with lowered levels of income inequality, greater wealth should result in changing individuals' preferences for democracy. It does so in this case through its effects on inequality.

Important individual-level assumptions are implicit in all three of these hypotheses. Whereas the first and second hypotheses assume that individuals' preferences for democracy are related directly to their level of income – support for democracy rises as individuals become richer – the third hypothesis proposes a more indirect relationship: higher incomes overall tend to go together with reductions in inequality, which helps advance individuals' preferences for democracy.

Verification for these individual-level assumptions is not readily available, however. In particular, it needs to be ascertained whether preferences for democracy are guided by calculations of economic reward. An instrumental logic underlies at least two of the three hypotheses reviewed: Poorer people care less for democracy because they have more to lose and less to gain from it; richer people fear the consequences for their incomes that democracy and progressive taxation might have in more unequal societies.

Demonstrating that concern for democracy may not be related directly to present and expected material well-being will result in throwing open the search for other causal mechanisms. Perhaps it is not material preferences that drive the observed relationship between development and democracy. It might be that "poor countries are too poor to afford a strong state" (Przeworski et al. 2000: 166). Democracies grow and prosper where state institutions are stronger and better resourced; thus, strengthening institutions (and not enriching individuals) may provide a more promising pathway for strengthening democracy (Geddes 1994; Hiskey and Seligson 2003; Remmer 1997). Or it might be that there is no direct *causal* connection between economic development and democratic stability (Remmer 1993), and as Przeworski (2004) suggests, the robust correlation observed between them may be accounted for better by specific historical antecedents. These large and competing claims are worthy of separate detailed investigations. In this chapter, I have a narrower and more manageable objective.

I examine specifically whether the link from economic development to democracy works via the intermediation of individual preferences and individuals' behaviors. With the help of evidence that I collected in sixty-one villages of rural north India, I test (a) whether poorer individuals have less faith in democracy, (b) whether poorer individuals suffer a shortfall in political efficacy that can limit their stakes in the democratic system, (c) whether poverty goes together with lower participation rates, and (d) whether concern for democracy among both richer and poorer individuals is related directly to the extent of income inequality within the community.

In these ways I examine the pathways through which differences in material well-being can potentially result in people caring less for democracy. First, with the help of a standard set of survey questions, I examine directly whether relatively poorer individuals support democracy to a lower extent. It may be possible, however, that the effects of poverty are more indirect. For instance, richer people with more resources may feel more confident about obtaining rewards from a democratic system, whereas poorer people may experience feelings of inefficacy and helplessness and thereby feel less of a stake in democracy. I examine differences in political efficacy scores in order to check for this second possibility. Third, even if they have equal faith in democracy and do not suffer from shortfalls in political efficacy, other limitations imposed by poverty in terms of time and resources may simply disable poorer people from participating equally actively. Indeed, evidence of lower participation rates observed within Western democracies has formed the core of the supposition that poorer people everywhere might care less for democracy. Examining differences in participation rates helps to check against this third possibility. Fourth, because it has been proposed that income inequality can mediate individuals' support for democracy I examine differences in support for democracy among villages with higher and lower levels of inequality. I look at average support scores among all residents of these villages. I also look separately at scores recorded by richer villagers.

Data collected in these sixty-one north Indian villages in the year 2004 helped to check whether poverty levels have any immediate association, directly or indirectly, with concern for democracy. It is possible that material well-being and inequality levels act on individual preferences with a time lag, perhaps because values, attitudes, and perceptions are slow to change. Using data that I had collected in the same villages in 1997, I check to see whether poverty and inequality as they existed seven years ago are any better reflected in villagers' support for democracy at the present time.

Data

Part of the reason that the proposed links between poverty and individual preferences for democracy have not been directly studied has to do with the paucity of data on poverty at the individual level. Such data are especially not available for newer democracies. Aggregate national data provide information about how poverty has increased or decreased overall in poorer countries, but individual-level data have to be constructed afresh in order to test the links at this level between poverty and democracy.

Assessing poverty is a complex undertaking.[1] Cross-national measures, such as $1 per day per capita, are error prone and travel poorly (Reddy and Pogge 2002; Wade 2004). Other measures, including the official Indian measure, based on daily calorific intake, are also difficult

---

[1] Poverty is multidimensional. Different aspects, including social deprivation and exclusion, in addition to material need, are implicit in different usages of this term. Here, I am focused narrowly on the material dimension of poverty. Sen (1999) presents a broader and more complex notion.

to administer and can yield conflicting estimates.[2] Such measures are also quite distant from people's own conceptions of poverty and well-being. They examine "deprivation and poverty ... not by the changing and varied wants and needs of poor [households themselves], but by the more static and standardized wants and needs of professionals" (Chambers 1988: 6). Quite different conclusions can emerge when poverty in a region or community is viewed with the help of these two different lenses. As Jodha's (1988: 2421) seminal study notes: "households that have become poorer by conventional [i.e., the professionals'] measurement of income in fact appear better off when seen through different qualitative indicators," based on concepts and categories that these households themselves use for assessing changes in economic status.

The hypothesized links between individual poverty and democratic preferences require that the person concerned should feel himself or herself poor – else, he or she might not experience so acutely the putative tradeoffs between higher income and greater commitment to democracy. It is better, therefore, while testing these assumptions, to work directly with a lived conception of poverty, one that reflects the experiences and worldview of the people whom one studies.[3]

Such a local conceptualization of poverty was utilized for this exercise, which assessed relative material status for households currently resident in sixty-one village communities of Rajasthan, India. The sixty-one villages studied here were selected originally in 1997 for another study (Krishna 2002). Because these data from seven years ago were available, field research was undertaken in the same villages between May and July 2004. The mix of villages selected in 1997 in five dissimilar districts of this state is representative of different patterns of rural settlements that exist in this area. Some villages are located

---

[2] For instance, altering the recall period in the officials' household from thirty days to seven days can result in *halving* the proportion of people living in poverty (Lal, Mohan, and Natarajan 2001; Sen and Himanshu 2005).

[3] Mattes, Bratton and Davids (2003) constructed a "lived poverty index" for a similar exercise that they conducted in six countries of sub-Saharan Africa. Their method also employs a contextually relevant definition of poverty, which is quite different, however, from the scale of measurement used by me in India.

close to market towns and major roads, whereas others that are more remotely located and harder to access; single-caste-dominant villages are represented in the mix along with mixed-caste villages; and large villages are included along with smaller ones.

The Stages-of-Progress methodology was utilized in each village for grading households' material status. This methodology has been employed before for two other investigations undertaken in this geographic area and also for other investigations undertaken in Kenya, Uganda, and Peru. It is described briefly below in terms of the following successive steps:[4]

Step 1. Assembling a representative community group separately in each village. We took particular care to ensure that all members of the village community, particularly poorer and lower status villagers, were present at these meetings.

Step 2. Presenting our objectives. We introduced ourselves as researchers, and we made it clear that we did not represent any program agency, government, or nongovernmental organization (NGO), so there would be no benefits or losses from speaking freely and frankly to us. We mentioned these facts in order to remove any incentives people might have for misrepresenting the poverty status of any household in their village.

Step 3. Defining "poverty" collectively. Community groups in each village were asked to delineate the locally applicable Stages of Progress that poor households typically follow on their pathways out of poverty. What does a household typically do, we asked the assembled villagers, when it climbs out gradually from a state of acute poverty? Which expenditures are the very first ones to be made? "Food," was the answer invariably in every village. Which expenditures follow immediately after? "Sending children to primary school," we were told without any hesitation or disagreement. As more money flows in incrementally, what does this household do in the third stage, in the fourth stage, and so on?

Lively discussions ensued among villagers in these community groups, especially in relation to the tenth and higher stages. But the

---

[4] For more details on this methodology, see www.pubpol.duke.edu/krishna

TABLE 3.1. *Stages-of-Progress*

1. Food for the family	
2. Send children to school	
3. Some clothes to wear outside the house	
4. Start repaying debts	
5. Replace thatch roof	*Poverty Cutoff*
6. Dig a well	
7. Purchase cows or buffaloes	
8. Construct a *pakka* (brick) shelter	*Prosperity Cutoff*
9. Purchase ornaments	
10. Purchase radio, tape recorder, refrigerator	
11. Purchase motorcycle	
12. Purchase tractor or car	

answers that they provided particularly about the first eight stages of progress were essentially the same across all sixty-one villages.[5] Next, we asked the community group to define a commonly understood poverty cutoff. After crossing which stage is a household no longer considered poor, we asked the assembled villagers. This poverty cutoff was commonly placed after Stage 5 in all sixty-one villages. Households that have crossed past the first five stages are no longer regarded as poor in this region, and households that have failed to make this grade are considered to be poor both by themselves and by others in these communities.

Clearly understood and commonly shared criteria for classifying households as poor or non-poor were derived in each village. Table 3.1 presents these stages and the poverty cutoff.

It is hardly surprising that communities sharing common economic and cultural spaces should, in fact, report a common set of aspirations, represented in the locally applicable stages of progress that poor households typically follow on their pathways out of poverty. Poverty is an objective condition that is experienced subjectively. More than a condition, it is a relationship – between a person and his or her

---

[5] The first five stages were similar in all sixty-one villages. Stages 6 to 8 were also exactly the same in fifty-five of sixty-one villages. In the remaining six villages the identification of these stages was the same, though some differences arose in their ordering.

possessions and between this person and other persons. Like other relationships, poverty is socially constructed and collectively defined. The Stages of Progress provide a device to get closer to such a locally shared definition of poverty as well as a criterion for identifying who is poor and who is not.

Step 4. Treating households of today as the unit of analysis, inquiring about households' poverty status today and seven years ago. A complete list of all households resident in each village was prepared. Referring to the shared understanding of poverty developed in the previous step, the assembled community groups were asked to describe each household's status at the present time and separately for seven years ago.[6] Following this determination it was possible to assign each household to one of four separate categories: Very Poor (Stages 1 through 3); Poor (Stages 4 and 5); Medium (Stages 6 through 8); and Well-to-do (Stages 9 and above). It was also possible to classify households similarly in terms of their material status of seven years ago.

Two separate variables are available for analysis: Stage2004 refers to a household's material status in the year 2004, whereas Stage1997 refers to its material status in 1997. The four categories – Very Poor, Poor, Medium, and Well-to-do – were also constructed separately for 1997 and 2004.

In addition, it is also possible to consider transitional categories – those who fell into poverty between 1997 and 2004 (not poor in 1997 but poor in 2004), and those who rose out of poverty over the same period of time (poor in 1997 but not poor in 2004). These transitional categories are particularly important for examining hypotheses related to the effects that adverse economic circumstances have on individuals' preferences for democracy.

Step 5. Interviews with a random sample of households. Stages indicated by the community groups for each household were cross-checked with individual members of a random sample of households. From among the total number of 11,403 households resident in these villages, a random sample of 2,291 households was drawn for conducting interviews.

---

[6] Household composition has been relatively stable in these villages. Relatively few households, less than 2 percent in all, had either migrated in or migrated out permanently in these villages during the seven-year period considered for the study.

Members of 1,731 of these 2,291 households had also been inter-viewed in a separate investigation conducted in 1997 in the same villages. These individuals, originally selected through random sam-pling, were re-interviewed, and another 560 interviewees were selected, once again through random sampling.[7] A pre-tested questionnaire was administered, concerned with asset holdings, attitudes toward democ-racy, participation in political activities, and political efficacy, in addi-tion to socioeconomic information.[8]

Of the 2,291 households interviewed in 2004, 14.1 percent are Very Poor (Stages 1–3), 37.8 percent are Poor (Stages 4–5), 28.8 percent are Medium (Stages 6–8), and 19.3 percent are Well-to-do (Stage 9 and higher). A close correspondence exists between a household's present material status and its possession of various assets. Average landhold-ings increase progressively: Very Poor households possess 3.5 bighas of land on average; Poor households have 5.7 bighas; Medium house-holds have 8.1 bighas; and Well-to-do households possess 11 bighas of land on average.[9] Livestock herds increase in regular increments as households move up these categories, and type of dwelling also improves in steady increments.

Recall information about households' situations seven years ago closely matches assets actually possessed at that time. For the subgroup of households that were also interviewed in 1997, stages of progress for 1997 (as recalled in the community meetings of 2004) are closely correlated with assets actually possessed in 1997 (as recorded in the survey conducted in 1997).

---

[7] Individuals were selected for interviews in 1997 through random sampling of the most recent voters list. Frequent competitive elections have helped make these lists complete in their coverage, and I did not meet any adult villager whose name was not on the voters list. The study in 2004 undertook repeat sampling with refreshments for 560 in-dividuals who were not available at the time of interviews. A total of 33 selected individuals refused to be interviewed. Additional replacements were selected for these individuals. No differences in socioeconomic characteristics exist between the 1,731 repeat and the 560 first-time interviewees: age, gender, caste status, landholding size, and education levels are similarly distributed within both categories of respondents.

[8] The Stages-of-Progress methodology has more steps in addition to the ones mentioned here. These additional steps are intended to ascertain specific reasons that are associ-ated, respectively, with individuals' descents into and their escapes from poverty.

[9] A bigha is the local unit of measuring agricultural land. One bigha is approximately equal to one-sixth of a hectare.

The Stages-of-Progress methodology provides a reliable benchmark for assessing how high up the ladder of material prosperity a particular household has climbed within this region. It also provides a useful database for testing various hypotheses related to the individual-level relationship between poverty and democracy.

Faith in Democracy

Faith in democracy as a system of governance does not appear to be significantly different among villagers with different levels of material well-being. The purported tradeoff between consumption (necessities) and democracy (a supposed luxury) that forms a key part of the hierarchy-of-needs hypothesis is not supported by the attitudes expressed by more than two thousand villagers.

Following Rose and Haerpfer (1998), survey questions proposed concrete tradeoffs between a democratic option and a non-democratic one. Other surveys (such as the Afro- and Latino-Barometers) were also consulted for guidance on appropriate questions. A range of such questions was asked of all respondents in order to ascertain their support for democracy.

Pre-testing these questions and all others in this survey helped to ascertain that these questions were relevant and easy to comprehend, that alternative responses exhausted the range of possible answers, and that there was sufficient variation in responses to justify including the particular question. Answers to a sample of questions are reproduced in the tables that follow.

Question S1: Suppose a government leader arranges to increase your monthly income by five hundred rupees for all times, but asks in return that s/he stay in power forever, i.e., there will be no more elections and democracy will be ended. Will you support this leader and this arrangement?[10]

Table 3.2 provides the range of responses given by different categories of respondents. Although Very Poor villagers are a little more

---

[10] Five hundred rupees (approximately $12) is equal to almost half the monthly income of poorer people in these villages. An alternative version of this question referred to a 50 percent increase in monthly income, but there was no significant difference in responses by any of the four categories of respondents. I thank Adam Przeworski for suggesting the initial wordings of these two survey questions.

TABLE 3.2. *Support Ending Democracy in Exchange for a Permanent Income Increment*

	Strongly Support	Support	Neither Support nor Oppose	Oppose	Strongly Oppose
Well-to-do	3.5%	12.3%	20.9%	47.2%	16.1%
Medium	3.0%	13.4%	20.8%	52.5%	10.3%
Poor	2.4%	16.5%	17.3%	51.9%	11.9%
Very Poor	4.0%	15.7%	17.3%	52.2%	10.9%

Mantel-Haenszel chi-square: 1.2052, Prob: 0.2723; $n = 2,214$.

likely to support or strongly support the antidemocratic arrangement compared to Well-to-do villagers (19.7% v. 15.8%), these differences are not statistically significant, as the chi-square test results show.[11] A roughly similar proportion of villagers in each category opposed this arrangement. Responses to other survey questions also tend to confirm this impression of there being no significant difference in support for democracy between richer and poorer villagers.

Question S2: If the political party that benefits you loses the election and still wishes to remain in power, would you support its bid to stay in power undemocratically?

Table 3.3 gives the range of responses. Although 55.4 percent of Well-to-do villagers said that they would oppose or strongly oppose the non-democratic alternative, a somewhat higher percentage of Poor and Very Poor villagers, respectively, 63.2 percent and 59.2 percent, are opposed or strongly opposed. Once again, these differences are not statistically significant.

Question S3: We should get rid of parliament and elections and have a strong leader decide things. Do you agree or disagree with this statement?

Table 3.4 provides these results. No differences are apparent between the four different categories of villagers in relation to this particular non-democratic alternative. Faith in democracy (or its alternative)

[11] Frequencies in each cell were used to calculate this statistic. Cell counts in this table and the ones considered later are all ten or higher.

TABLE 3.3. *Support Favoured Political Party Staying in Power Despite Losing Election*

	Strongly Support	Support	Neither Support nor Oppose	Oppose	Strongly Oppose
Well-to-Do	3.0%	21.4%	20.3%	47.9%	7.5%
Medium	6.0%	18.1%	14.5%	48.2%	13.2%
Poor	3.8%	18.9%	13.2%	54.4%	8.8%
Very Poor	3.0%	19.6%	18.3%	53.0%	6.2%

Mantel-Haenszel chi-square: 1.12, Prob: 0.294; $n = 2,270$.

does not differ depending on the wealth category of the respondent. Individuals who support democracy on any one of these three measures also tend, by and large, to support it on the other two measures. Later, I will report the pooled responses to all three of these questions.

Other standard survey questions related to trust in democratic government were also asked of these respondents. These answers were also not significantly different between relatively richer and relatively poorer villagers. Villagers were asked whether they agreed or disagreed with the following statements (1) No opposition party should be allowed to compete for power; (2) The military should come in to govern the country; and (3) When hiring someone, even if a stranger is more qualified, the opportunity should be given first to relatives and friends. A nearly equal proportion of villagers from all four categories disagreed or strongly disagreed with each respective statement.

Although villagers value democracy quite highly as a *system* of government, they are less sanguine about the functioning of the

TABLE 3.4. *A Strong Leader Should Decide Things and Parliament/Elections Should be Abolished*

	Disagree or Strongly Disagree
Well-to-do	74.5%
Medium	72.4%
Poor	78.3%
Very Poor	76.6%

TABLE 3.5. *How Much Public Money Do People in Government Waste?*

	Waste a Lot of Public Money	Waste Some but Not a Lot	Waste Little Money	Waste No Money at All
Well-to-Do	42.7%	36.7%	15.2%	5.1%
Medium	36.2%	40.8%	18.6%	4.3%
Poor	57.1%	29.3%	11.3%	2.2%
Very Poor	44.0%	34.6%	17.3%	4.0%

Mantel-Haenszel chi-square: 0.1115, Prob: 0.7385; $n = 2,177$.

government itself. Democracy is supported by the vast majority of villagers, rich and poor alike; simultaneously, there is widespread cynicism about government agents' performance on a day-to-day basis.

Question S4: Do you think that people in the government waste a lot of public money, waste some of it, or don't waste very much of it?

Table 3.5 gives the range of responses for each of the different economic categories considered. More than three-quarters of all respondents in each category considered that government officials waste some or a lot of public money. Once again, no statistically significant differences separate the four categories of villagers.

To the extent that one can rely on survey data – and although the survey method is hardly foolproof, it is not clear what other technique should be used for this purpose – relatively poorer villagers and relatively richer villagers do not exhibit any appreciable differences in terms of support for democracy or faith in democratic government. They are equally and strongly supportive of democracy as a system of government, and they are equally cynical about the government of the day and about government officials.

What about those who have recently fallen into poverty? Does their reversal of fortune get reflected in significantly different attitudes toward democracy compared to other villagers? In order to investigate this question, I conducted the above analyses afresh considering transitional categories – those who fell into poverty between 1997 and 2004, those who rose out of poverty over the same period of time,

TABLE 3.6. *Support Ending Democracy in Exchange for Permanent Income Increment (transitional categories)*

	Strongly Support	Support	Neither Support nor Oppose	Oppose	Strongly Oppose
Poor in 1997 and 2004	3.0%	21.4%	20.3%	47.9%	7.5%
Escaped from Poverty	6.0%	18.1%	14.5%	48.2%	13.2%
Fell into Poverty	3.8%	15.1%	13.2%	60.4%	7.6%
Not Poor in Either Year	3.0%	13.6%	18.3%	53.0%	12.2%

Mantel-Haenszel chi-square: 1.214, Prob: 0.283; $n = 2,212$.

those who were poor in both years, and who were not poor in both years. Table 3.6 reports the results of responses to Question S1.

Combining figures for those who are Opposed and Strongly Opposed, we find that a total of 68 percent of those who fell into poverty are in opposition to the non-democratic option – compared to 61.4 percent of those who rose out of poverty, and 65.2 percent of those who were not poor in both years.[12] Those whose economic fortunes have taken a downturn are apparently *not* about to abandon their support for democracy.

Material poverty (and even recent impoverishment) does not, therefore, appear to be a significant separator between those who support and those who do not support democracy. These impressions are reinforced when additional results are considered, related to other aspects of engagement with democracy.

Political Efficacy

Richer people with more resources feel more confident about obtaining rewards from a democratic system, it has been suggested; whereas poorer people experience feelings of inefficacy and helplessness. Perhaps the link between poverty and lack of support for democracy works via the route of political efficacy (Abramson 1983; Almond and Verba 1965; Conway 2000; Lipset 1981; Schur, Shields, and Schriner 2003; Verba and Nie 1972).

---

[12] However, these differences are not significant as the chi-square test shows.

To test this hypothesis, five questions were included in the household survey, which have been used in the past to compare individuals' levels of political efficacy. Two questions relate to internal efficacy and three to external efficacy (Rosenstone and Hansen 1993; Verba et al., 1997). Respondents were asked whether they strongly agreed (scored 1), agreed (scored 2), disagreed (scored 3), or strongly disagreed (scored 4) with each of the following statements.

E1. I feel I do not have the ability to participate in politics.

E2. Sometimes politics and government seems so complicated that a person like me cannot really understand what is going on.

E3. Things are run by a powerful few, and ordinary citizens cannot do much about it.

E4. People like me don't have any influence over what the government does.

In addition, a fifth question asked:

E5. Do you think if you were to make contact with a government official or political leader, will you get a response (scored 2) or will you be ignored (scored 1)?

Individuals' responses to these five questions are closely correlated with one another, with higher scores on any one question going together generally with higher scores on each of the other four questions. Factor analysis shows that responses to all five questions load highly on a single common factor, indicating that there is a single common tendency underlying the five separate responses.[13] Because these five separate responses are so closely aligned with one another, it seemed legitimate to combine them within a single index.

The Political Efficacy Index was derived by adding together the five separate responses after first converting each response to a standardized range from 0 to 1, so that each response has an equal weight in the index. This 5-point aggregate was then transformed to

---

[13] Factor loadings on the single common factor are, respectively, 0.76, 0.77, 0.69, 0.74, and 0.61. Communality = 2.68, indicating that 67 percent of the combined variance is explained by the single common factor.

have a range from 0 to 100, which makes it easier to interpret regression results. Mean score on this Index is 32.1, and standard deviation is 27.1. Among all 2,205 individuals for whom scores on this Index were computed,[14] 406 individuals (18 percent) achieved the lowest score, 0 points, and another 31 individuals have the highest score, 100 points.

It remains to be determined whether relative material well-being makes the difference between high and low political efficacy scores. Apparently, material well-being would seem to matter: average political efficacy scores are 26 points for the Very Poor category, 31 points for Poor, 33 points for Medium, and 35 points for the Well-to-do category.

The effects of material well-being must be isolated, however, from those induced by other influences on efficacy. For instance, Delli Carpini and Keeter (1996) and Verba et al. (1997) show how gender matters for political efficacy and political participation. Women have consistently lower efficacy scores than men in these studies. Age has also been found to be associated positively with political efficacy (Abramson 1983; Bennett 1986; Rosenstone and Hansen 1993). Race is considered important in the American context (Bobo and Gilliam 1990; Verba et al., 1997), and its counterpart, caste, is regarded to be associated with political activity in the context of India (Mayer 1997; Jaffrelot 2003; Sheth 1999).

In addition to these variables – wealth, age, gender, and caste – about which relatively little can be done through policy intervention, at least in the short term, a second set of variables has also been identified in analyses of political efficacy and political participation. For instance, education has also been seen to matter, independently of material wealth (Finkel 2002; Jackson 1995, 2003; Seligson et al. 1995; Wolfinger and Rosenstone 1980). Information has been shown to matter apart from education (Bimber 2003; Dahl 1989; Delli Carpini and Keeter 1996; Ferejohn and Kuklinski 1990; Iyengar and Kinder 1987; Norris 2000). Social capital and social networks have also been found to be significant for efficacy and participation levels (Krishna 2002;

---

[14] Missing entries account for the remaining 86 individuals.

Paxton 2002; Putnam 1995; Rosenstone and Hansen 1993). Finally, individuals who feel excluded because of lack of access are also likely to experience a lower sense of political efficacy, thus access to government agencies through the agency of party officials or other intermediaries is also important to consider (Friedman 2002; Kohli 1987, 1990; Manor 2000; Mitra 1991; Vilas 1997).

Regressing the Political Efficacy Index on a first set of variables, including gender, age, poverty status, and caste, shows that material well-being is significant for political efficacy. Model 1 in Table 3.7 shows this first set of associations. The variable, gender, is a binary 0–1 variable, which takes the value 1 for females and 0 for males. Similarly, the three caste variables also take the value 1 if the respondent belongs to the respective caste group and 0 otherwise.[15] The material well-being variables are also 0–1; for example, the variable Very Poor takes the value 1 if the respondent's household belongs to this category and it is 0 otherwise. Medium serves as the control category, against which the other three categories, Very Poor, Poor, and Well-to-do are compared.

All of the variables considered in Model 1 are significant for the analysis of political efficacy. Material well-being is significantly and positively related to political efficacy, and gender, age and caste status also matter significantly. R^2 is only 0.09, however, indicating that quite an inconsiderable part of variation in political efficacy scores is accounted for by the variables considered in this analysis.

Other independent variables also need to be considered. These variables were measured as follows. Education is measured in terms of number of years of schooling. Information has a somewhat different construction than is usually found in the literature. It is measured here in terms of the number of sources (out of eight) that the respondent consulted over the past thirty days. These sources include family

---

[15] Scheduled Caste (SC) refers to the former untouchables, and Scheduled Tribe (ST) refers to what are, loosely speaking, India's aborigines. These categories are recognized by India's constitution, which provides schedules listing specific castes and tribes as SC and ST, respectively. Backward Caste (BC) is a more recent administrative listing, and it refers to caste groupings that are neither upper caste nor listed in the schedules for SC and ST. A total of 888 BCs, 278 SCs, and 371 STs were interviewed, along with 754 upper castes.

TABLE 3.7. *OLS Regressions on Political Efficacy with 100-Point Political Efficacy Index as the Dependent Variable*

	Model 1	Model 2
Intercept	35.4****	0.63
	(3.0)	(4.65)
Gender	−8.0****	−2.04
	(1.11)	(1.32)
Age	−0.13***	−0.00
	(0.03)	(0.04)
Material Well-Being		
Very Poor	−3.86**	−1.93
	(1.67)	(1.68)
Poor	−2.95*	−2.72
	(1.54)	(1.71)
Well-to-Do	7.54****	0.33
	(1.89)	(2.11)
Caste		
Scheduled Caste (dummy)	−5.07**	−2.85
	(1.90)	(2.09)
Scheduled Tribe (dummy)	−12.10****	−5.29*
	(1.80)	(2.10)
Backward Caste (dummy)	−5.22***	−2.22
	(1.34)	(1.49)
Education		1.99****
		(0.24)
Information		2.69****
		(0.37)
Social Capital		0.17***
		(0.05)
Access		
Political Party		1.01*
		(0.46)
Village Leader		5.58****
		(0.89)
N	2,157	1,814
R^2	0.09	0.32
F-value	25.57	45.42
F-probability	<0.0001	<0.0001

Note: Standard errors are reported in parentheses.

$^*p \leq .05.$ $^{**}p \leq .01.$ $^{***}p \leq .001.$ $^{****}p < .0001.$

members, neighbors, and village leaders, and also radio, TV, news-papers, the village assembly, and government officials.[16] On average, villagers consult 4.4 sources; standard deviation is 2.8.

Social capital is a village-level variable that measures, following Putnam (1995: 67), "features of social organization such as networks, norms and social trust that facilitate coordination and cooperation for mutual benefit" of the village community. A locally relevant index of social capital was developed earlier for villages in this region (Krishna 2002). This 100-point index, which combines responses to six separate survey questions related to membership in networks and norms of trust, reciprocity, and solidarity was utilized for this exercise.[17] Because respondents in each village were selected randomly, the average of their response scores is an unbiased estimator of village social capital. Mean village score on 100-point index of social capital is 59.3 points, and standard deviation is 12.0 points.

Two access variables were constructed. The variable, political party, was constructed by asking respondents whether they felt they could consult some political party official if they needed to make a con-nection with some government agency. The variable, village leader, was similarly constructed in reference to village leaders who could provide respondents with access to government offices. In both cases, "Yes" responses were coded as 1, and "No" responses were coded as 0.

---

[16] More usually, the information variable is constructed by assessing respondents' gen-eral knowledge about political matters; for example, Verba, Schlozman, and Brady (1995: 554) ask whether respondents know the names of their senators and con-gressmen, what the Fifth Amendment accomplished, and so on. Not surprisingly, this type of information variable is closely correlated with respondents' education levels. The information variable considered here – which examines sources consulted by less educated villagers (such as family members, neighbors, and village assembly) along with sources consulted by more educated ones (such as newspapers) – has a correlation coefficient with education of 0.29, enabling a concurrent evaluation of education and information.

[17] Responses to these six separate survey questions are closely correlated with one another, and in factor analysis they load commonly on a single underlying factor; thus, it is legitimate to combine them within an index. Factor loadings are all 0.68 or higher.

These two access variables are not significantly correlated with any of the material status variables or with any other independent variable. In addition, neither the information variable nor the education variable is closely correlated with material well-being. The rank-order correlation between Information and Stage is 0.35 and that between Education and Stage is even lower, 0.22. Correlation among other independent variables is also quite low, and the value of the Condition Index for the regression model reported in Table 3.7 is 21.2, which indicates low collinearity.

When these other independent variables are also included within the analysis, R^2 improves considerably. However, material well-being loses its earlier significance. None among the three material well-being variables is significant in the analysis of Model 2. Among the three caste status variables, only scheduled tribe is significant. Age and gender also lose their earlier significance.[18] On the other hand, education, information, social capital, and the two access variables are all significantly associated with higher political efficacy scores. Controlling for these variables eliminates the significance of material well-being.

Material status at the present time is not, therefore, a significant influence on political efficacy. It is not clear that poorer people face any shortfall in political efficacy that can limit their stakes in the democratic system.

It could be that material well-being acts on preferences and values with a time lag. In order to test this hypothesis, the lagged variables VeryPoor1997, Poor1997, Medium1997, and Well-to-do1997 were constructed based on households' poverty status of seven years ago. Regression analysis was undertaken afresh using these variables (in place of variables representing households' current poverty status). However, the regression results did not change in terms of which variables gained significance. As before, none of the material well-being variables is significant, and education, information, social capital, and access are all significantly associated with higher political

---

[18] Verba, Burns, and Schlozman (1997) similarly find that the gender variable does not achieve significance when other influences on efficacy are also simultaneously considered.

efficacy scores. Political efficacy is not related with levels of material well-being either at the present time or in the earlier period.

Participation in Democracy

Evidence examined so far has shown that faith in democracy is not significantly different between relatively richer and relatively poorer villagers. Political efficacy levels are also not significantly related to material well-being, especially after controlling for other important influences. Quite similar findings are obtained when participation rates are examined in the following.

Participation rates are measured here in the usual manner, considering responses to seven separate survey questions related to campaigning, canvassing, contacting, and protest. These questions are:

P1. During the last *Vidhan Sabha* (State Assembly) election campaign, did you talk to any people and try to show them why they should vote for one of the parties or candidates?

P2. Did you go to any political meetings, rallies, speeches, etc., in support of a particular candidate?

P3. Did you do any (other) work for any one of the parties or candidates during that election?

P4. How much did your own work in the campaign contribute to the number of votes that the candidate got in your village – a great deal, some, very little, or none?

P5. How often in the past year did you get together with others in this village and jointly petition government officials or political leaders?

P6. What about the local *panchayat* (village assembly) leaders? Have you initiated contact with such a person in the last twelve months?

P7. In the past two years, have you taken part in any protest march or demonstration on some national or local issue?

Individuals' responses to these seven separate questions are closely correlated with one another. Factor analysis shows that responses to all seven questions load highly on a single common factor, indicating that there is a single common tendency underlying the seven separate responses.[19] Because they all point commonly in the same direction, these responses were combined, after first being standardized on a 0–1 scale, to constitute a 100-point Index of Political Activity. Average score on this scale is 29.2 points, and standard deviation is 27.2.

Relatively poorer villagers, have lower average political activity scores compared to relatively richer villagers. Very Poor villagers scored an average of 23 points on the Index of Political Activity, Poor villagers scored 29 points, Medium villagers scored 33 points, and Well-to-do villagers scored 35 points on average. In addition, a significant association between participation and material well-being is ascertained when only a small group of socioeconomic variables is considered in regression analysis (Table 3.8, Model 1).

The variable, Stage, which represents a household's material status, is highly significant in the analysis of Model 1.[20] Gender, age, and two of the three caste status variables are also significant.

The variable, Stage, loses significance, however, when other independent variables are also considered in the regression analysis (Model 2).[21] Information, education, social capital, and the two access variables are all significantly associated with higher political participation.[22] Gender and one of the two caste variables (scheduled

---

[19] Factor loadings on the single common factor are all 0.68 or higher. Communality = 4.5, indicating that 64 percent of the combined variance is explained by the single common factor.

[20] The variable stage takes values from 1 through 12. It is used here, instead of the earlier dummy variables (Very Poor, Poor and Well-to-do). Alternative regression analyses considering these three dummy variables in place of stage did not produce any qualitatively different results.

[21] Political efficacy is not included here among the independent variables, because the relationship between efficacy and participation is complex and may even be circular. Although Verba, Schlozman, and Brady (1995) and Verba, Burns, and Schlozman (1997) demonstrate the links leading from efficacy to participation, Finkel (1985, 1987) validates the reverse causation, from higher participation to greater efficacy. Because of these possible two-way links, I elected to analyze participation and efficacy separately.

[22] The fact that access is so important suggests that participation may be induced as well as autonomous. With the data at hand I am unable to distinguish the relative contribution of these separate motivations.

TABLE 3.8. *OLS Regressions on Political Participation with 100-Point Index of Political Activity as the Dependent Variable*

	Model 1	Model 2
Intercept	28.6****	−24.3****
	(3.0)	(5.91)
Gender	−9.5****	−4.67**
	(1.2)	(1.46)
Age	−0.08*	0.02
	(0.04)	(0.04)
Stage	1.6****	0.37
	(0.27)	(0.31)
Caste		
Scheduled Caste (dummy)	0.09	1.69
	(2.19)	(2.39)
Scheduled Tribe (dummy)	−9.1****	−1.84*
	(2.03)	(2.40)
Backward Caste (dummy)	−2.73*	−1.45
	(1.56)	(1.71)
Education		0.88**
		(0.29)
Information		3.54****
Social Capital		0.28***
		(0.06)
Access		
Political Party		2.55****
		(0.66)
Village Leader		8.91****
		(0.99)
N	1,745	1,301
R^2	0.09	0.27
F-value	28.2	24.75
F-probability	<0.0001	<0.0001

Note: Standard errors are reported in parentheses.

$^*p \leq .05.$ $^{**}p \leq .01.$ $^{***}p \leq .001.$ $^{****}p < .0001.$

tribe) are also strongly (and negatively) associated with participation scores. However, material well-being (as indicated by Stage) loses its significance in the analysis.

Poverty does not go together thus with significantly lower participation rates. Given education, information, and access, poorer individuals participate in democratic politics at the same rate on average as wealthier individuals.[23]

Once again, in order to test whether poverty status has a lagged effect on participation rates, perhaps because values and culture are slow to change, the variable Stage1997 was used in regression analysis in place of poverty status at the present time. Once again, the regression results did not change in terms of which variables gained significance.

Poor people do not participate significantly less, therefore, when other important influences are also considered in addition to relative wealth. In the context of the United States, Bobo and Gilliam (1990) show similarly that respondents' race and family income are not significant influences on participation when controls for education and political knowledge are included in the analysis. Schur, Shields, and Schriner (2003) also show that household income is not a significant influence; whereas education and civic skills are significantly associated with higher participation rates.[24]

Neither faith in democracy nor political efficacy or participation rates show evidence of support for the hypothesis that poor people's concern for democracy is significantly lower than that of relatively richer people. Individuals' concern for democracy does not appear, therefore, to provide the micro-level link explaining the macro-level association between economic development and democracy.

Inequality and Attitudes

Does reduced inequality provide a better micro-level explanation for changes in individual preferences leading to greater concern for democracy? Recall that the theory is that economic development reduces

---

[23] It might be that there is a particular self-selecting subgroup of individuals who (a) more actively seek out information, education, and access, and (b) also participate more actively in politics. This alternative explanation cannot be ruled out with the data at hand. The fact, however, that any such subgroup includes *both* richer and poorer individuals implies, once again, that material well-being is not a significant separator between politically active and inactive citizens.

[24] This result holds in their analysis for the group of people who do not have physical disabilities. For people with disabilities, not surprisingly, possessing a car acts as a significant influence on participation, thus higher income levels matter.

income inequalities. Lower inequality is, in turn, related to greater support for democracy, particularly among relatively richer individuals who fear that democracy results in redistribution of wealth. The untested micro-level assumption is that individuals, particularly relatively richer ones, prefer democracy more in societies where inequality is lower.

A partial test of this assumption is provided by the data at hand. We have figures for inequality in each of sixty-one village societies where this study was undertaken. If the assumption is valid, then individuals' preferences for democracy – particularly among richer villagers – should be higher within villages where inequality is at a lower level.

Two different inequality variables were considered alternatively for this part of the analysis consisting, respectively, of standard deviation (within each village) of landholding size and standard deviation of households' Stages at the present time. Two separate dependent variables were also considered. The first dependent variable, faith in democracy, was put together by consolidating responses for all respondents in each village to three survey questions, S1–S3, listed earlier (the first three questions asked in relation to faith in democracy). A second dependent variable, faith among Better-Off villagers, was constructed in the same way but only for relatively richer villagers, those currently located at Stage 6 or higher.

Table 3.9 presents regression results when the first dependent variable, faith in democracy, is examined, which considers average responses for all respondents in a village. Notice that the inequality variable utilized here, standard deviation of landholdings, is not significant for this analysis. Separately, the other inequality variable (standard deviation of Stages) was also found to be not significant. The same five variables that were significant in individual-level analysis of political efficacy and participation rates – education, information, social capital, and the two access variables – are once again significant when faith in democracy is examined at the village level.

Two other independent variables were also considered here, which relate to some other expectations expressed by modernization theorists. The variable distance to market is a surrogate for relative

TABLE 3.9. *OLS Regressions on Faith in Democracy with
100-Point Index of Faith in Democracy as the Dependent
Variable*

	Coefficient	Standard Error (S.E.)
Intercept	51.6****	11.2
Inequality		
Std. Dev. of Landholding	−0.04	0.08
Information	8.01****	1.67
Education	3.6***	0.89
Social Capital	0.28**	0.13
Access		
Political Party	11.65****	1.33
Village Leader	4.02**	1.92
Distance to Market	0.07	0.06
Infrastructure	0.29	0.18
N	60	
R^2	0.71	
F-value	17.31	
F-probability	<0.0001	

$*p \leq .05.\ **p \leq .01.\ ***p \leq .001.\ ****p < .0001.$

commercialization. It measures the distance in kilometers to the nearest market town. The variable infrastructure measures on a 12-point scale the quality of road, electricity, and water supply facilities available in each village. Higher commercialization and better links with markets and urban areas should result in providing higher support for democracy, according to Apter (1965) and Lerner (1958). None of these variables is significant, however, in regression analyses conducted on the dependent variable, faith in democracy, indicating that modernization theory's tenets might not apply very well within this context.

Separately, regression analysis was undertaken using faith among better-off villagers as the dependent variable, but the results did not change in terms of which variables gained significance. Differences in inequality levels among different village societies do not find reflection in any perceptible differences in average support for democracy – either among all villagers or even among the subset of relatively richer villagers.

Like values, however, perceptions of inequality might be relatively slow to change, and attitudes at the present time might carry over from inequality levels of the past. Because we have both recall data on Stages of seven years ago and data on the actual landholdings at that time, we can check to see whether inequality as it existed seven years ago is any better reflected in villagers' support for democracy at the current time. Re-doing the regression analysis using the lagged standard deviations of landholding and Stages does not change the nature of results observed in Table 3.9. The lagged inequality variables are not significantly associated with any of the two dependent variables, respectively, faith in democracy and faith among Better-Off villagers. The null hypothesis cannot be rejected, therefore, that inequality levels (within communities) are not associated at the individual level with support for democracy.

This hypothesis might need to be tested additionally with data from larger aggregations of individuals: people's inferences about inequality and their expectations about redistribution may be drawn from contexts wider than their own immediate environment. It is unlikely, however, that inequality in one's proximate surroundings will not be at least partly reflected in these wider calculations; one's immediate neighbors stand most to gain from redistribution of land, for instance. Still, lacking data for a wider context, the results shown here are presented as a partial test of the inequality hypothesis.

Conclusion

Assumptions about individuals' preferences and behavior are implicit in some theories put forward to explain why higher wealth goes together with stronger democracy in a country. Support (or refutation) for these individual-level assumptions has proved hard to find hitherto. Lack of data on individuals' well-being levels – and even more so, lack of data on poverty *matched* with data on individuals' political attitudes and behaviors – has been the most important reason why these assumptions have not been tested, particularly among newer, poorer, and potentially unstable democracies.

The original database constructed here has shown that individual's concern for democracy is not directly related to levels of material deprivation.[25] Even when they do not derive significant material benefits, people in these villages continue to express strong support for democracy.

Findings similar to those reported here have also been provided by investigations conducted in Africa and other parts of South Asia. Poor Africans consulted by Bratton and Mattes (2001a: 108) "overwhelmingly support democracy and reject authoritarian regimes." Even though they are not happy with the way that democracy actually works for them in terms of material benefits, most Africans are committed to democracy for intrinsic as well as instrumental reasons (Bratton and Mattes 2001b). The majority of African respondents were not satisfied with their own economic conditions, yet "more than two out of three Africans interviewed say that democracy is 'always preferable' to non-democratic forms of government" (Afrobarometer 2002: 2). In Nepal, one of the poorest countries of the world and also one where the experience of democracy has been deeply dissatisfying in terms of tangible results, more than three-fourths of a national sample of more than four thousand respondents, including richer and poorer citizens, "retain their trust in democracy [and] . . . clearly reject non-democratic alternatives" (Hachhethu 2005: 68).

It is not peculiarly India where individuals' preferences for democracy are not tightly linked with present or expected material status, although the experience of more than fifty years of nearly uninterrupted democracy may have something to do with reinforcing non-instrumental preferences for democracy in India. Even in India, however, lack of access prevents people from engaging more effectively with democracy. Access matters, as we saw earlier, for efficacy, participation, and support for democracy. Individuals who gain access through the agency of political parties or local leaders are more likely to participate at higher rates, and they also feel themselves more efficacious politically. Improving access through strengthening institutions

---

[25] Because levels of material well-being are not strongly correlated in these villages with levels of education, information, social capital, and access, the four variables that are significantly associated with higher political efficacy and higher participation scores, even indirect connections between poverty and concern for democracy are not established in this context. See Norris (2002: 93–5) for more on this distinction between direct and indirect effects of wealth.

might be key, therefore, to making democracy stronger and more accessible by all. Education and information are also critical to this task. They matter for participation, support, and efficacy in these north Indian contexts, and they also matter equally in other contexts of democracy.[26]

Accountability is essential to reduce the likelihood of domination, and minimizing domination is a central objective of democracy (Shapiro 2003). Individuals provided with better access and armed with information and education can much better hold their governments accountable – not just at election time but also on a more regular basis. Concern for and engagement with democracy is in large part a consequence of how legitimate and accountable the system is regarded to be (Hiskey and Bowler 2005). Stronger preferences for democracy should arise as the risks of domination and neglect get abated in this manner and as the system is more widely perceived as being legitimate and fair.

Whether long experience with democracy reinforces individuals' preferences; whether access provision and institution building are more important to this task; whether education and information are most important; or whether all these aspects matter to some degree will need to be ascertained more carefully through separate contextually valid inquiries. It cannot be assumed, however, that poorer individuals or residents of poorer countries care any less for democracy than their better-off counterparts.

---

[26] Bratton and Mattes (2001a) demonstrate the importance of education and information for democracy in an African context. Finkel (2002), Hiskey and Seligson (2003), and UNDP (2004) do so for different Latin American contexts.

4

Inequality and Democracy in Latin America

Individual and Contextual Effects of Wealth on Political Participation

John A. Booth and Mitchell A. Seligson[1]

Seymour Martin Lipset in *Political Man* (1960: 28) made the classic statement that "most countries which lack an enduring tradition of political democracy lie in the underdeveloped sections of the world." With respect to Latin America, the region of the world on which we focus, Lipset used numerous indicators of national wealth that led him to characterize Latin American nations as economically

[1] This study draws on the continuing series of surveys collected by the Latin American Public Opinion Project (LAPOP) at Vanderbilt University, affiliated with the Center for the Americas at Vanderbilt. The 2004 series of surveys used in this chapter were funded with the generous support of the United States Agency for International Development (USAID). Margaret Sarles, Bruce Kay, and Eric Kite in the "Office of Democracy and Governance" of USAID, supported by Maria Barrón in the Bureau for Latin America and the Caribbean, secured the funding. Critical to the project's success was the cooperation of the many individuals and institutions in the countries studied. These include, for Mexico, Jorge Buendía and Alejandro Moreno, Departamento de Ciencia Política, Instituto Tecnológico Autónomo de México (ITAM); for Guatemala, Dinorah Azpuru and Juan Pablo Pira, Asociación de Investigación y Estudios Sociales (ASIES); for El Salvador and Honduras, Ricardo Córdova, Fundación Dr. Guillermo Manuel Ungo (FUNDAUNGO), José Miguel Cruz, Instituto Universitario de Opinión Pública (IUDOP) de la Universidad Centroamericana, UCA, and Siddhartha Baviskar, University of Pittsburgh; for Nicaragua, Luis Serra and Pedro López Ruiz, Universidad Centroamericana (UCA); for Costa Rica, Luis Rosero-Bixby, Universidad de Costa Rica, and Jorge Vargas, Programa Estado de la Nación; for Panamá, Marco A. Gandásegui hijo, Centro de Estudios Latinoamericanos (CELA) and Orlando J. Pérez, Central Michigan University; for Colombia, Carlos Lemoine, Centro Nacional de Consultoría (CNC), and Juan Carlos Rodríguez-Raga, University of Pittsburgh. Polibio Córdova, CEDATOS/Gallup, Ecuador, provided excellent guidance on sample design for all of the teams. We thank the graduate assistants at the University of

94

underdeveloped.[2] He found that economic underdevelopment was associated with either unstable democratic government or dictatorship. He classified two-thirds of Latin American nations as stable dictatorships at the time of his study in the late 1950s. A special drag on democracy, he argued, was insufficient education. The effects of inadequate education, he argued, took their toll at the micro (i.e., individual) level, rather than at the level of nations as entities. Since that classic work was published more than forty years ago, numerous studies have tested the development–democracy link, and many (but not all) have confirmed it.

More recent work by Przeworski et al. partially refuted the relationship that Lipset uncovered, finding no impact of economic development on the probability of the inauguration of democracy (Przeworski et al. 1996). Nonetheless, that research did find that economic development is not, after all, irrelevant for democracy because Przeworski and his coauthors found that it has been a sine qua non for the survival of democracy once it is established. They demonstrate that democracies simply do not break down once they have surpassed a certain minimum economic threshold. Moreover, among countries that have not surpassed a minimum level of economic development, breakdown is more likely when economic growth falters.

Today, however, we encounter scenarios that make the development–democracy association worth revisiting. First, despite their relative poverty, most Latin American countries, in a transformation widely noted, have become – at least formally – electoral democracies (Huntington 1991; Peeler 1998; Smith 2005; Vanhanen 1997). Thirteen of the region's nations are now classified as "free," and eight

---

Pittsburgh who were responsible for auditing the quality of the data that we received from each country team: Miguel García, Sawa Omori, and Rosario Queirolo. At Vanderbilt University, Dinorah Azpuru, Abby Córdova and Daniel Moreno were responsible for cleaning the merged database. Miguel Gómez, formerly of the Universidad de Costa Rica, provided excellent advice on the questionnaire design. Finally, we wish to thank the 12,401 individuals in these eight countries who took time away from their busy lives to answer our questions. Without their cooperation, this study would not have been possible.
[2] An early empirical confirmation of Lipset's thesis is Martin C. Needler. 1968. Political Development and Socioeconomic Development: The Case of Latin America. *American Political Science Review* 63: 889–97.

"partly free," with only Cuba and Haiti remaining "not free."[3] As Robert Pinkney (2003: 157) argues, "When Lipset was writing in 1959 ... it seemed plausible to believe that only a few wealthy countries possessed the necessary qualifications for membership in the democratic club.... Yet the transitions we have witnessed since the 1980s indicate that some of the world's poorest countries can gate-crash the club." And, as Peter Smith (2005: 52) contends: "Over time, the association between economic development and political democracy lost its empirical force."

On the other hand, the contrasting case of Venezuela comes to mind, a country that had far surpassed the Przeworski threshold for democracy long before President Hugo Chávez successively weakened the quintessential institutions of liberal democracy by neutering the legislature and largely undermining judicial independence. Venezuela's growing petroleum-based wealth notwithstanding, the sharp reversals of most elements that define liberal democracy in that country force one to wonder whether the impact of crossing the economic development threshold for democracy determined by Przeworski and his colleagues is quite so irreversible as they believed. Indeed, if one agrees with Przeworski's classic definition (as we do) that democracy is the "institutionalization of uncertainty," it would appear that Venezuela is no longer a democracy. That is, it is difficult to imagine that Chávez could effectively be voted out of power, and that he would allow an opposition government to take over. Recent developments in Bolivia and Ecuador, where leftist-populist presidents have called constitutional conventions that they hope will emulate many of same kinds of measures instituted by Chávez, suggest serious challenges to the institutions of liberal democracy in those countries as well. More generally, although nearly all Latin American nations have progressed economically since the 1960s (Nicaragua and Haiti being the two key exceptions), many remain poor by the standard of the advanced industrial democracies, having GNPs per capita of only one-tenth or less than those of rich nations, raising again the question as to how it is that poor nations can emerge as democracies.

---

[3] Freedom House, *Country Report*, 2005, http://freedomhouse.org/template.cfm?page= 21&year=2005 (accessed December 25, 2006).

The dramatic expansion of democracy worldwide, and particularly in Latin America, and the various challenges to Lipset's research, raise the key question we examine here: Are economic development and democracy linked, as Lipset and others have argued? Or, at least in the case of Latin America, are development–democracy links largely, if not entirely, absent, as Smith has concluded? More specifically, if there once was a link between economic development and democracy in Latin America, is there any clear evidence that wealth still drives democracy or is related to democratic development in Latin America today? Our aim in this chapter is to revisit the question of the impact of wealth/poverty on democracy by examining eight Latin American nations at both the micro- and macropolitical levels. We do so in ways different from most prior research. We seek to untangle the macro effects of wealth/poverty at the national or contextual level and at the micro level of individual wealth/poverty in shaping the political involvement of citizens.

Nearly all of the prior studies that we cite in this chapter (see the endnotes) have focused heavily on system-level democracy, and examined system-level wealth as the key predictor. Among the relatively small number of studies that look at democratic behavior at the individual level, however, system-level variables have been almost always ignored. Indeed, most individual-level studies have been either single-country studies, in which system level variables (such as economic development) are therefore a constant, or multi-nation studies in which individual characteristics have been aggregated, thus erasing the link between system-level characteristics and individual-level behavior.[4] To move beyond prior research and simultaneously capture systemic and individual-level variables, we use data from an eight-nation survey of Latin American nations that, on their face, confirm Lipset's macro-level finding – that system-level democracy (both recently and over time) is stronger in wealthier nations and in countries that have had more long-term economic growth over the last fifty years (see Table 4.1). Our first macroeconomic variable is per capita gross domestic product (GDP) in purchasing power parity (PPP) terms. It measures relative

---

[4] For a discussion of the problems that aggregation of individual-level data create, see Seligson 2002.

TABLE 4.1. *Bivariate Correlations with System-Level Democracy Measures*

	Mean Vanhanen Index of Democracy for 1900—1989	Freedom House Combined Index for 2003 (Polarity Reversed)[a]
Macro-Level Measures		
PPP Income 2002	.490	.565
GDP Growth 1950–2000	.316	.475
Micro-Level Measures		
Wealth of Individuals	.307[**]	.303[**]
Individual Educational Attainment	.151[**]	.151[**]

[a] Freedom House combined scores for 2003 with polarity reversed so that greater freedom is indicated by a higher score.
[**] Relationship significant at the .01 level.

national economic wealth by determining the mean level of economic activity in each nation per person. The second macroeconomic variable is the total percentage increase in national GDP from 1950 to 2000. This variable captures each nation's long-term improvement in national economic performance.

There is also evidence from surveys in those eight nations (Table 4.1) that the wealth and educational levels of *individuals* may be linked both to higher level systemic democracy scores over the very long run (1900–1989) and to the current level of democracy.[5] Because we have recent identical survey data from eight adjacent Latin American nations that are quite varied in terms of their wealth and democracy scores, we can examine some of the questions raised by Lipset's observations and by the political and economic evolution of the region. In Table 4.1, the individual wealth measure is an index we have constructed from

[5] Note that the individual-level data correlations with system-level traits are used in Table 4.1 for illustration only. There are problems, both statistical and logical, with this sort of simple correlational analysis that we discuss at greater length later, including the possibility that other factors intervene to generate spurious relationships. Indeed, we demonstrate in the following that by controlling for intervening variables and using appropriate statistical techniques, these individual-system correlations are essentially spurious.

our survey respondents' reporting of having various articles of wealth: potable drinking water, indoor plumbing, television sets, refrigerator, cell phone, automobiles, washing machine, microwave oven, and computer (range 0–14). Educational attainment refers to the total number of years of formal education reported by survey respondents. Indeed, our linked and identically designed surveys allow us to explore the question in more detail than Lipset was able to,[6] having to rely as he did on disparate contextual measures and virtually no cross-national survey data from countries in the developing/democratizing world.

Lipset's main focus is on system-level democracy, but he also emphasizes individual characteristics as important. To have argued otherwise would have meant that Lipset believed that the micro-level results were merely spurious, a position he explicitly rejects. He contends, instead, as cited in Chapter 1 of this volume, that the wealth–democracy relationship is indeed the same as at the system level – that more wealth enables more and better citizen participation and therefore helps ensure democracy. To bolster his argument, Lipset cites Aristotle's argument from *The Politics* that a democracy requires low levels of poverty that would allow the population to participate intelligently in politics and avoid demagogic appeals. This view, skeptical of the prospects for democracy in poor societies, Lipset grounds in evidence he cites from various countries indicating that working class individuals tend to be more authoritarian and to vote for antidemocratic parties. On the other hand, there are other scholars who have argued that there is much less to fear in the participation of the poor. Indeed, Krishna and his co-authors have found a wide variety of highly *democratic* forms of participation among the poorest members of society (Krishna 2002; Krishna, Uphoff, and Esman 1997).

A strong case can be made that individual participation, including working class participation, is the essence of democracy, a term that literally means citizen participation in rule. One of the most finely argued and historically grounded studies supporting that view is

---

[6] Although the sample and questionnaire designs for all eight countries were identical, question modules covering country-specific issues (e.g., post conflict concerns in Guatemala and violence in Colombia) were included in the surveys. Those country-specific modules are not analyzed here.

that of Rueschemeyer et al. (1992), who show that the emergence of autonomous working class forces, especially unions, in Latin America was essential to the development of democracy in the region. Sorensen goes further still, arguing that it was economic crisis and the failure of the authoritarian economic development model in the 1980s that led to the citizen participation that contributed to the collapse of authoritarian regimes. Booth, Wade and Walker attribute the democratic transitions in Central America in the 1980s and 1990s to the collapse of the region's growth boom in the mid- and late-1970s, which served to mobilize working and middle class forces who utilized civil society organizations to strike out against authoritarian regimes (Booth, Wade, and Walker 2006; Cohen 1973; Pateman 1970; Rueschemeyer et al. 1992; Sorensen 1993.) There is ample evidence for Latin American, then, that at the macro level, economic growth may stimulate non-elite social sectors that challenge antidemocratic elites; whereas subsequent economic slowdown may challenge the regime with political crises that can lead to greater democracy.

In considering micro-level forces, research by the authors of this chapter nearly three decades ago found fragmentary evidence from several Latin American nations that did not support the conventional wisdom, derived from studies of the advanced industrial democracies, that associated wealth with more citizen political participation.[7] In that research we mostly lacked the luxury of national probability samples from a wide variety of countries, and instead relied largely on a series of special-purpose samples of regions, villages, or selected occupational groups. Even so, we reported then that based on our limited evidence, in contrast to better-off urban dwellers, Costa Rican peasants participated significantly *more* in organizations and community projects. Other studies, similarly based on limited samples or in some cases descriptive evidence and other evidence from the largely predemocratic era in Latin America, also reported political participation among the poor and working classes including peasants, urban workers, and rural women. These findings were surprising given the largely

---

[7] Booth 1978, 1979; Booth and Seligson 1978a; Bourque and Warren 1979; Cornelius 1974; Fishel 1979; Landsberger and Gierisch 1979; Moore 1979; Seligson 1978.

authoritarian and often repressive contexts of most of the countries in the region at that time.

One finding, based on a study of peasant involvement in politics by Landsberger and Gierisch, was striking: "At the level of participation as an individual phenomenon, one outstanding finding has been, quite simply, its high quantitative level. There is no hint here of the passive, apathetic peasant" (Landsberger and Gierisch 1979: 95). These studies suggested that even the rural poor in Latin America harbored considerable capacity to act in democratic ways and, thus, to contribute positively to democracy or the democratization process. At the same time, however, those studies systematically suggested that elites were likely not heeding the demands of the poor, a situation that could (and indeed did) ultimately lead to challenges of political legitimacy and potential unrest (Adams 1979).

This chapter undertakes a fresh look at the issues of the economic development/economic status–democracy linkage by carrying out a comparative eight-nation analysis. We study six different dimensions of participation in those eight nations and use both individual-level and system-level characteristics to test the Lipset thesis. We find weak to nonexistent evidence to support Lipset's thesis that it is wealth at the system and individual level that drives participation. What we find, instead, is that economic development and wealth are far less powerfully linked to participation than Lipset had suggested. We conclude the chapter wondering about the implications of this participation for democratic consolidation.

Methodology

We are fortunate to have in our study a sample of countries on which key system-level variables vary considerably; we can also control for major historical/cultural variables. All of the countries in our sample were former colonial dependencies of Spain, all went through long periods of dictatorship/military rule, and all emerged as democracies at some point in the twentieth century.[8] In each of the countries,

---

[8] There is a myth that Costa Rica has always been democratic, but, as Booth (1998) and Lehoucq and Molina Jiménez (2002) clearly show, that is not true.

TABLE 4.2. *Inter-Country Variation on Key Economic and Democratic System-Level Variables**

	Freedom House Combined Index, 2003, Reversed	Cumulative Percent GDP Growth from 1950–2000 from Penn World Tables	Gross National Income per Capita, 2002	Infant Mortality per 1,000
Mexico	10	192	$5,920	24
Guatemala	6	82	$1,760	36
El Salvador	9	57	$2,110	33
Honduras	8	14	$930	32
Nicaragua	8	−18	$710	32
Costa Rica	11	138	$4,070	9
Panama	11	202	$4,020	19
Colombia	6	144	$1,820	19
Sample mean	8.63	101.38	$2,668	25.50

* See Appendix 4.A for sources.

Catholicism has been the dominant religion, although in recent years evangelical Christian groups have made substantial inroads in some of the cases, especially Guatemala. Finally, the economies of these countries were long dependent on agricultural export commodities, although over the past few decades there have been important shifts into more diversified and modern production modes.

The data in Table 4.2 demonstrate the similarities and differences in our set of eight Latin American nations. We employ Freedom House's (FH) two basic measures to capture the national level of democracy (Freedom House 2005a). Freedom House scores nations from 1 (best) to 7 (worst) on two scales – political rights (elections, pluralism, participation), and civil liberties (freedom of expression, associational rights, rule of law, individual rights). We invert the polarity on these scales (range from 0 to 6 each) and add them together to provide a 12-point measure of democracy. We reversed the countries' scores so that (more conveniently for our analysis) a higher value indicates greater democracy. Country scores on our revised FH democracy measure range from a high of 11 for Costa Rica and Panama to a low of 6 for Guatemala and Colombia. In terms of the growth of GDP in the second half of the twentieth century, the countries range from a high of 202 percent in Panama to a *negative* 18 percent in Nicaragua. Per capita incomes range from a high of nearly $6,000 in Mexico to a low of $710 in Nicaragua. Finally, infant mortality, a good negative measure of national social development, varies sharply from its low levels in Costa Rica (where it approximates infant mortality rates in the United States) to a rate four times as high in Guatemala. In short, at the macro-level, these countries present wide variation in levels of development and democracy, but they share common historical, economic, religious, and cultural backgrounds.

Sample Design

A study of the impact of inequality on democratic participation must gather data on the values of *all* citizens, not just the active ones, the politically "important" ones, or those who live in major towns and cities. Surprisingly, however, many studies carried out in Latin America that claim to represent the views of the nation, are often based on samples that systematically underrepresent certain sectors of the population.

The database for this chapter was designed to be fully representative of the voting-age population of each of the countries included in the study. The target group of countries was eight contiguous nations of northern Latin America nations as shown in Figure 4.1. In this study, we determined that a sample of 1,500 respondents per country would satisfy our objectives. Below the level of the nation, each stage of sample selection was done following probability proportional to size (PPS) criteria so that the probability of any one unit being selected was in direct proportion to the most recent population estimates. At the level of the individual country, the confidence interval would be about ± 2.5 percent; whereas for the pooled sample, which is what we use for this analysis, the confidence level is less than 1 percent.[9]

---

[9] Probability sampling techniques link the accuracy of the estimate of the actual characteristics of the population sampled to the size of the sample, rather than to the population size of the universe, in this case our eight countries. Effectively, then, the

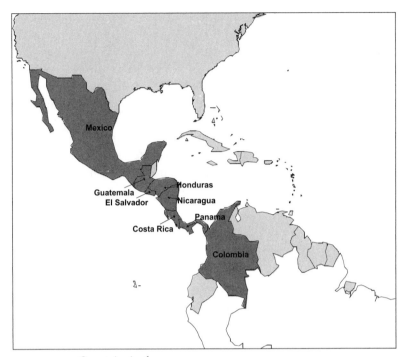

FIGURE 4.1. Countries in the survey.

The sample design involved multistage stratification. The overall sample was thus first stratified by country, and then substratified within each country by major geographic region in order to increase the precision of the results. We divided each country into a minimum of five regional strata, representing the major geographic divisions of the countries. In that way, we could ensure that all of the major regions of the country would be represented. We were careful not to exclude remote regions; in Honduras, for example, we developed an English version of the questionnaire for use on the Bay Islands so as not to

---

more respondents in a survey, the better the chance there is for an accurate reading (smaller confidence interval) irrespective of the total population. Thus, for the pooled eight-nation sample, with 12,000 respondents, the likelihood of an accurate reading is better than for any single national sample with 1,500 respondents.

exclude that population from the survey. Similarly, we developed translations of the questionnaire in five Mayan languages for Guatemala. Careful translation and pre-testing was employed to assure the comparability of the items and their referents regardless of the language employed.

To further increase the precision of the samples, we subdivided each of the country-level strata into urban and rural. We know that many other similar samples in Latin America largely exclude rural areas because of their inaccessibility, but we did not because the inclusion of the rural poor was essential to testing the economic development/participation thesis. We relied on census definitions of urban and rural and divided our within-country regional strata so that each one would faithfully represent the urban/rural breakdowns within them. At the level of the nation, as noted, we used samples of the same size (ca. 1,500) so that each nation would have an equal weight in the overall results. Because the actual sample size by country deviated somewhat from 1,500, we have introduced a post hoc weighting factor to correct for this small variation. The next stage in the sample design involved determining the neighborhoods – primary sampling units or PSUs – in which the interviews would take place. Using census maps from each country's respective census bureaus and using population data segments, we randomly selected the maps from within each stratum and then randomly selected the segments in which the interviews would be carried out. In that way, voting-age adults in each country had an equal and known probability of being selected. Thus, respondents living in sparsely populated rural villages had the same probability of being selected as respondents in large cities.

The final stage involved a systematic selection of housing units within a PSU (using the census maps and locally updated information). We set a cluster size of eight interviews in each urban PSU and twelve in each rural PSU. We allowed the larger clusters in rural areas because of the far lower housing density compared to urban areas and the increased cost in travel time that the larger number of rural clusters would imply. Once the household was selected, we determined that random selection of the respondent within the household was far too costly because it would have required multiple callbacks, effectively impossible in rural areas. Thus, we decided to use a quota sampling methodology at the level of the household. The quotas were established for age and sex, again based on the most recent census data for each country.[10]

Dependent Variables

We conceptualize political participation broadly, taking our cue from Lipset's argument that those who may take part more broadly and more effectively may avoid the pitfalls of demagoguery. We draw on theoretical arguments that participation is much more than voting (Cohen 1973; Pateman 1970), and the precedent of research demonstrating that participation is multidimensional (Booth and Seligson 2005; Verba and Nie 1972; Verba, Nie, and Kim 1971). There is also strong evidence that political participation in Latin America is multidimensional (Biles 1978; Booth 1976; Booth and Seligson 1978b; Booth and Seligson 1979; Booth and Seligson 2005), and we wanted to capture that dimensionality. Our political participation variables are:

> **Voting:** This index combines measures of the respondent reporting being registered to vote and having voted in the immediate past presidential election.

[10] The sample design also considered the prospect that some selected households could be empty ("blanks") or that selected respondents might refuse to cooperate leaving us with a smaller sample size than we had planned. As a result, in each country an estimate of non-coverage was included. The final samples are shown in the following table. As can be seen in the table, the total pooled sample N was 12,401. In the analysis section we explain how we produced results taking into account this complex sample design.

Country	Sample Size	Percent of Entire Sample
Mexico	1,556	10.1
Guatemala	1,708	11.1
El Salvador	1,589	10.3
Honduras	1,500	9.7
Nicaragua	1,430	9.3
Costa Rica	1,500	9.7
Panama	1,639	10.6
Colombia	1,479	9.6
Total	12,401	100.0

Contacted a public official: The respondent reported having contacted or not contacted each of three types of public officials: a legislator, ministry official, or local government official.

Communal activism: The respondent reported helping to solve a community problem within the last year, as well as donating money, contributing work, attending meetings, and organizing a new group to solve a problem.

Civil society engagement: This index provides a mean score for respondent's intensity of meeting attendance for four types of civil society organizations – church-related, school-related, community improvement, and a professional, business or producers.

Campaign-partisan activism: The respondent's reported engagement in having tried to persuade someone else how to vote, and his/her frequency of attendance at the meetings of a political party.

Protest involvement: The respondent's reported frequency of participation in public protests.

See Appendix 4.A for operationalization and data index construction details.

Independent Variables

We employ two indicators of an individual's personal poverty/wealth, as explained earlier. One is **personal wealth** as measured by the respondent's standard of living. The measure we use is an index reflecting the possession of artifacts of wealth in the respondent's household, including indoor plumbing, various electrical appliances, computers, automobiles, and so on.[11] We also include the number of years of **education**

---

[11] We could have used respondent monthly income as a measure of personal wealth and resources, but decided not to because about 10.5 percent of the respondents declined to answer this question, giving us missing data problems. The measure of personal wealth (as personal artifacts), in contrast, has no missing data. Second, income is not distributed the same way as personal wealth. Heads of households tend to be principal income earners. Their spouses and dependents may largely derive their standard of living from the income of the principal income earner without earning much income of their own. Nevertheless, these dependents enjoy the benefits of

completed. Education, a critical resource for individuals, is a crucial item in Lipset's analysis and has been shown to correlate significantly with political participation variables in almost every circumstance. (See Appendix 4.A for more details.)

We use three contextual variables indicative of the wealth and resources existing within the larger politico-economic context. Our first system poverty/wealth variable is a measure of the overall economic activity per capita, **gross national income per capita (PPP)** in the year 2002. The second – and negative – measure of system wealth is **infant mortality** per 1,000 live births at the time of the survey, which is indicative of the extent to which the national government invests or fails to invest in healthcare for its citizens (World Bank 2002).

A third contextual resource measure is an ordinal indicator of the relative size and degree of urbanization of the community of residence of the respondent, which we call *size of respondent's community of residence*, which captures the degree of urbanization. This item is an ordinal measure of the relative population size/urbanization of the city/town/village in which the respondent's interview took place, ranging from the national capital or metropolitan area (scored at 5) down to small town or rural area (scored as 1). We include it for several reasons. Throughout Latin America, urban areas are systematically wealthier than rural areas,[12] but there are aspects of urbanization that are not picked up directly in the other variables we have included for analysis. We have in mind the density of urban services, including health, telecommunications, transportation, the media and the like that provide a level of resources to urban residents that can far surpass those of rural areas. There are, of course, costs of living in urban areas (crime, pollution) that might depress participation. Indeed, fear

---

personal wealth and, thus, are likely to have attitudes and behaviors that correspond to the income category of the household's principal income earner. The Pearson's bivariate correlation between monthly income and personal wealth in our sample is .632. In order to avoid potential collinearity problems in our regression models and to avoid lost cases, we opted to use wealth rather than income.

[12] Indeed, for this pooled sample, there is a strong positive correlation between the size of the community and the level of wealth, the personal income, and the education of respondents. Means for each of these are significantly higher for each successively larger size of community.

of crime, as Putnam has noted, could help explain depressed participation in the larger cities, as it seems to do in the United States (Putnam 2000). Thus, we include, as a further means to test the Lipset thesis, this measure of urbanization as an index of wealth and development represented by proximity and access to these key resources. It is coded to reflect the relative size of the place in which the interview was conducted. As constructed, it does not directly measure levels of service provision, relative ease of contacting officials, nor the difficulty of collective action, but we use it as a reasonable surrogate for all three.

In general, governmental personnel and resources tend to concentrate in larger communities. We believe this should be an asset to the residents of cities by making public officials easier to communicate with than it might be for rural and small-town dwellers. In contrast, some research indicates that the effect of community size on political participation works in the opposite way (Verba and Nie 1972). Participation may be easier rather than harder in smaller, more clearly bounded communities than in sprawling urban areas or large cities. We suspect, based on our previous research in Latin America, that residents of poor rural and smaller communities will have greater need to cooperate and seek the assistance of public officials and will therefore be more politically active than their urban counterparts.

Control Variables

Our research and that of others has shown that political legitimacy attitudes likely mediate citizen engagement in politics (Booth and Seligson 2005), so we include legitimacy norms in our model of citizen engagement as control variables. We wanted to be sure that we could control for legitimacy attitudes so that we could know whether the modes of political participation we were measuring (our dependent variables) were motivated by support for or frustration with the political system (Booth and Seligson 2005; Booth, Seligson, and Barrantes 2006).

In research done separately, we have identified multiple distinct legitimacy dimensions among Latin American citizens, based on their evaluations of various points of reference in the political system ranging from the abstract to the very concrete. We employed confirmatory factor analysis on multiple legitimacy items included in our 2004 surveys. These items were drawn from a wide array of legitimacy-related questions suggested by legitimacy researchers including Dalton, Norris, and Easton (Dalton 1999; Easton 1965, 1975; Norris 1999b: Introduction). The analysis revealed six distinct dimensions of political legitimacy (political support): political community, support for core regime principles, evaluation of regime performance, support for political institutions, support for local government, and support for political actors.[13] Although these six dimensions are weakly-to-moderately associated among themselves, they are by no means sufficiently overlapping to constitute the same construct. They, thus, capture quite different aspects of citizens' evaluations of their political systems. These six dimensions affect political involvement and other attitudes in distinctive ways.

We also include three demographic variables as controls: respondent's *sex*, *age*, and *age squared*. The age-squared variable is to account for the frequently encountered curvilinear relationship between age and participation, whereby the very young (for lack of interest and/or stake in the community) and the very old (owing to a diminished physical capacity to participate) engage less in politics. Using age squared enables us to model the curvilinear form of the age–participation relationship, and, thus, allows us to better test for its true effect.[14]

Analysis

Lipset's general hypothesis may be restated as follows: *Economic development/wealth should correlate positively with citizens' political*

---

[13] Once identified by confirmatory factor analysis, we used exploratory factor analysis of the variables that made up each legitimacy dimension to extract factor scores for each dimension. For purposes of this analysis, we converted the factor scores into a standardized measure ranging from 0 to 100. We then input missing data on the six dimensions using EM (expected maximization using maximum-likelihood estimation) method. See the chapter appendix for details on the indexes and items from which they were constructed.

[14] One technical matter concerns the possibility of multicollinearity (excessively high levels of association) among our independent variables, which could interfere with accurate regression results. To make certain there is no problem in this regard, we have calculated the simple bivariate correlations among all the independent variables. None of the bivariate pairs approaches a correlation of .60, a level indicative of multicollinearity.

participation. Or, expressed alternatively, *underdevelopment/poverty should associate negatively with citizens' political participation.* We have five measures of poverty/wealth: two are individual (personal wealth measured using an index of assets possessed and personal educational attainment measured in terms of numbers of years spent at school); two are assessed at the country level (GDP per capita and infant mortality); and one is assessed at the level of the respondent's place of residence (the ordinal variable for size of place of residence).

The most appropriate solution for data that include variables measured at the individual level, such as wealth and education, and variables measured at the national level, such as GNP and infant mortality levels, is to employ a multilevel statistical model, such as hierarchical linear modeling, but there are too few national cases for that technique to work while employing more than one context-level variable at a time. When performed, this analysis revealed that neither GDP per capita nor infant mortality rates are significant. Thus, national wealth – here operationalized directly as either overall national economic activity per head or indirectly as infant mortality rates – does not affect citizens' participation rates. Of course, with a larger sample of countries such effects might be found, but in our data, at least, we cannot detect them using hierarchical linear modeling.

Having confirmed that no significant system-level effects exist, we therefore employ ordinary least squares regression to analyze the remaining possible relationships between wealth and participation. Tables 4.3 and 4.4 present the results. It is important to note, however, that with pooled samples there needs to be some means to filter out the effects of respondents being in one country rather than any of the other seven countries. The best means for such a control is to employ national fixed effects variables (dummies), for example, scoring a Mexican citizen with a 1, all others with 0, and so on for each country.

Turning first to the micro level, if Lipset is correct, personal wealth (here measured as possession of consumer goods and artifacts indicative of standard of living) should correlate positively with political participation. Tables 4.3 and 4.4 reveal that the individual wealth variable, however, is not significantly positively associated with any of the six participation variables. Moreover, contacting public officials correlates significantly negatively with wealth – the poor contact more officials than do those who are better off.

TABLE 4.3. *OLS Regressions of Political Participation Variables on Individual and Systemic Wealth Measures*

Independent Variables	Voting		Contacting		Communal Activism	
	beta	Sig.	beta	Sig.	beta	Sig.
Wealth	.020	.111	−.043	.002	.000	.983
Education	.159	.000	.110	.000	.140	.000
Size of place	−.057	.000	−.090	.000	−.100	.000
Political community	.037	.000	−.001	.911	.017	.068
Regime principles	.027	.003	.062	.000	.024	.013
Regime performance	.008	.399	.008	.425	.004	.653
Institutions	.007	.457	.003	.769	.011	.280
Local government	−.008	.404	.083	.000	.078	.000
Political actors	.010	.312	−.018	.097	.001	.931
Gender	−.028	.001	−.047	.000	−.102	.000
Age	1.442	.000	.522	.000	.646	.000
Age squared	−1.185	.000	−.441	.000	−.532	.000
Mexico	−.005	.665	.008	.521	−.010	.427
Guatemala	−.125	.000	.007	.596	.041	.002
El Salvador	.015	.201	−.004	.762	−.007	.593
Honduras	.000	.982	−.061	.000	.062	.000
Nicaragua	.027	.035	.007	.621	.012	.356
Panama	−.065	.000	−.056	.000	.012	.352
Colombia	−.035	.004	−.039	.003	−.017	.185
R^2		.154		.040		.059
F		113.85		26.208		39.108
Model significance		.000		.000		.000
Number of observations		11,909		11,939		11,965

Note: Shading in grey indicates confirmation of Lipset's hypotheses; **boldface** indicates relationship significant at .05 or less.

On the chance that it is the infrastructural wealth of the community rather than individual or personal wealth that might shape participation, we consider the impact of the size of the respondent's community of residence variable. We note that – other factors held constant – residing in a larger community appears to lower rather than increase most forms of participation. The exception is protest behavior, which is significantly higher in larger cities than in small towns and rural communities.

TABLE 4.4. *OLS Regressions of Political Participation Variables on Individual and Systemic Wealth Measures*

Independent Variables	Civil Society Activism		Partisan-Campaign Activism		Protesting	
	beta	Sig.	beta	Sig.	beta	Sig.
Wealth	−.024	.070	.005	.719	.000	.975
Education	.075	.000	.123	.000	.153	.000
Size of place	−.055	.000	−.059	.000	.026	.018
Political community	.024	.008	−.045	.000	−.022	.017
Regime principles	.015	.107	.056	.000	.100	.000
Regime performance	.011	.225	.021	.033	−.008	.419
Institutions	.009	.356	.061	.000	−.016	.135
Local government	.072	.000	.050	.000	.039	.000
Political actors	.003	.808	−.031	.004	−.045	.000
Gender	.053	.000	−.086	.000	−.057	.000
Age	.904	.000	.349	.000	.081	.079
Age squared	−.819	.000	−.292	.000	−.027	.558
Mexico	−.032	.006	−.047	.000	−.004	.732
Guatemala	.139	.000	.012	.362	.015	.242
El Salvador	−.051	.000	−.035	.005	−.050	.000
Honduras	.164	.000	.028	.031	−.023	.083
Nicaragua	.059	.000	.033	.014	.060	.000
Panama	−.091	.000	.037	.004	.014	.254
Colombia	.009	.487	.039	.003	.102	.000
R^2		.106		.047		.071
F		74.03		30.77		46.67
Model significance		.000		.000		.000
Number of observations		11,940		11,964		11,609

Note: Shading in grey indicates confirmation of Lipset's hypotheses; **boldface** indicates relationship significant at .05 or less.

Lipset's hypothesis about political participation fares far better when the measure of individual resources employed is education. Educational attainment shows a significant positive relationship to all the participation variables. Lipset, then, was indeed correct that education is a resource for participation, a point supported by Vanhanen (1997). This finding also emerges equally clearly in other chapters of this volume. In our pooled sample, educational attainment is correlated with wealth, as one might expect; the simple bivariate correlation between

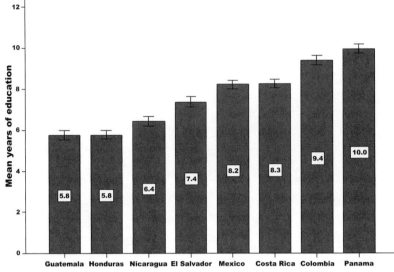

FIGURE 4.2. Mean Level of Formal Education Attained, by Country.

them is .58. Thus, whereas wealth and education are associated, only 33 percent of their variation is shared in these eight Latin American nations. This clearly demonstrates that, although correlated with wealth, minimal to moderate education is not exclusively a privilege of the wealthy elite in Latin America today. Figure 4.2 graphs the mean levels of education for each country. The range is from about six years of schooling in Honduras and Guatemala to almost ten years of formal education in Colombia.

In order to assess fully the impact of education on participation, we must examine the relative impact of different levels of schooling. If the less educated are much less politically active than the well-educated, it may be a very important factor in a country's democratic prospect. Our data reveal that the effect of education on participation, while significant, is limited. Figure 4.3 plots participation rates for voting, partisan-campaign activism, contacting, and protest participation. All four indeed reveal the expected increasing rates for progressively higher education levels, but the slopes of these lines are not very steep. That is

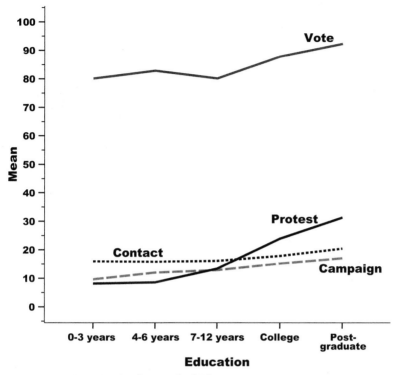

FIGURE 4.3. Participation by Level of Education.

to say that the participation differences between the most and least educated is modest. The results for civil society and communal activism, not shown for the sake of the simplicity of the graph, follow precisely the same pattern of small rather than large participation differences between the less and more educated.

To sum up, Lipset correctly predicted that the educated would be more politically active than the uneducated, but we find in our eight Latin American democracies that the impact of education is small rather than great. We do not encounter a politically hyperactive educated elite contrasting to a politically passive less-educated population. The more-educated take part only somewhat more. But the lesser educated citizenry also participates in politics and does so at rates only slightly less than the better-educated citizenry. The less-educated, thus, engage the political system through multiple channels, do so at rates only slightly less than their better-educated peers, and in no way constitute a politically passive population. We do not believe that these small differences in participation rates by education allow the conclusion that national-level democracy is a function of or depends solely on the educational attainment of the most-schooled citizenry.

A few other findings in Tables 4.3 and 4.4 warrant comment. Various legitimacy norms affect participation differently. Perceiving a sense of political community significantly elevates voting and civil society engagement, but reduces partisan-campaign and protest activity. Support for regime principles (that is, for democracy), elevates four types of participation – voting, contacting, party-campaign activism, and protesting. Most intriguing here is that protesting associates positively with support for democratic regime principles. The more they embrace democratic norms, the more citizens of these democracies are likely to protest. Thus, protesting is not a behavior associated with antidemocratic norms, but quite the opposite.

The legitimacy norm that most influences participation is the evaluation of local government's performance, which elevates every type of participation save voting. Thus, evaluation of the level of government that is most proximate to the voter – the municipality – evokes the greatest participation reaction. We suspect that it is the very proximity and familiarity of local government – which because it is less remote and powerful than national government – that encourages citizens into participating more in every mode but voting.

Women engage in civil society activism of the types we measure (primarily community-based) more than do men, but men are more active than women in all the other participation modes. Older citizens participate sharply more than younger ones for everything but protesting. Once age surpasses sixty, civil society activism tails off significantly.

In sum, at the micro level, we fail to detect any significant effects of wealth on political participation. In our eight contemporary Latin American nations, *greater individual wealth either decreases or fails to increase* five distinct kinds of political participation. Even more striking is that the poor actually engage in *more* partisan and campaign activism than those with more economic resources. With respect to the two macro-level variables analyzed using HLM (Heirarchical Linear Modeling) techniques there was no confirmation of Lipset's hypothesis concerning wealth and participation. For the context variable, size of community of residence, wealthier environments corresponded with less participation in five of six relationships, and the only positive association was for protesting. At the micro-social level, Lipset's expectation that greater personal wealth would generate more participation failed to be confirmed for all six participation modes. Indeed, the only significant relationship was a negative one for wealth and contacting public officials. So for these four measures of wealth, both contextual and individual, the overwhelming finding is that greater economic development, community wealth and personal wealth do *not* increase participation.

In contrast to these wealth measures, education functions somewhat as Lipset anticipated, but our findings indicate that the difference schooling makes in participation rates is modest. Education almost certainly conveys an advantage to citizens that boosts their political involvement, but it is not a drastic effect. So even though we have confirmed Lipset's expected positive education–engagement link, its actual impact is small. In our eight Latin American countries, the effect on participation of having more or less education appears to us to matter much less than Lipset's theory implies.

Democratic Norms
The primary focus of this chapter so far has been political participation. Other contributors to this volume have also addressed Lipset's hypothesis that greater wealth would also predict a deeper commitment to democracy. Stated inversely, he argued that a widespread presence of authoritarianism among the working classes and poor constitutes an obstacle to democracy in developing nations. To examine this proposition very briefly, we have replicated our analysis using two measures of commitment to democratic norms. One is a measure of support for basic democratic participation rights constructed from various items, and the other asks the respondent to place himself or herself on a continuum of agreement with the statements that "what we need in this country is a strong leader who doesn't have to worry about being

elected" versus "I prefer an elected leader as we have now" (a high score indicates a preference for elected leadership, a low score for an unelected strongman). For both of these measures of individual commitment to democracy, personal wealth has no significant impact, education contributes significantly and positively, whereas greater size of community of residence contributes negatively and significantly to democratic norms.[15] Although education contributes to higher democratic values, as Lipset predicted, its effect is quite modest – in particular, for participation. The well-educated are slightly more democratically inclined than the poorly educated, but both groups average on the strongly pro-democracy end of the scales for both measures. This demonstrates that, at least for our eight Latin American countries, Lipset was mistaken about the impact of personal wealth and systemic wealth on commitment to democratic principles. Although he was correct about the salutary effects of education, they are small effects, and both the schooled and unschooled support democracy. These findings dovetail neatly with those we reported for participation.

Conclusions

At the micro level, we have found a sharp disjuncture between the predicted impact of personal poverty/wealth and education on participation in contemporary Latin America. Poverty far less clearly reduces citizen political involvement than Lipset believed, and in some cases actually increases it. Nor do poorer citizens hold democratic norms much less than richer citizens. Education does enhance all types of citizen participation, but the difference it makes is modest.

On balance, then, data from in our eight countries reveal that Lipset's prediction that the poor would fail to take part in politics and would hold authoritarian values is incorrect. His hypothesis that education would elevate participation and commitment to democratic norms is true, but the difference it makes in contemporary Latin America is marginal rather than substantial. Modernization theory's central tenets that, at the micro-social and macro-social level, wealth and

---

[15] These results of OLS regression using the same independent and control variables as in Tables 4.3 and 4.4 are not shown to conserve space.

education are foundations of democracy thus do not stand up to empir- ical scrutiny. Latin Americans, poor or rich, are roughly equally polit- ically active and committed to democracy. Indeed, somewhat to our surprise, although education does affect participation rates, the effects are modest and commitment to democracy is high among both the less and more educated.

Were educational levels increased, citizen participation would likely rise somewhat. This might marginally increase government awareness of and responsiveness to the demands of the public. A modest increase in citizen commitment to democratic values resulting from higher levels of education might also marginally contribute to democratic consol- idation by further elevating the already high ratio of democrats to authoritarians. On the negative side, increased educational attainment would also likely bring a corresponding increase in the level of politi- cal protest, one of the participation modes most sensitive to education. This would not necessarily threaten democracy or support for democ- racy, but it could well increase levels of turmoil.

At the macro level, other factors held constant, we find no evidence that citizens in our eight Latin American nations are less likely to participate, or more likely to be authoritarians, when their economic systems are less developed. Moreover, except for protest, people are *more active in politics and more committed to democracy* when they live in smaller communities that are less endowed with services.

These findings are on balance quite contrary to Lipset's expectations and thus raise interesting questions. First, what are the implications of having poor citizens who are relatively active political participants? We have seen that although poverty has almost no effect on partic- ipation rates and democratic values, the less-educated population is, indeed, somewhat less active and somewhat more authoritarian. Are these very minor differences likely to predispose these systems toward authoritarian rule because the poor are active participants? We doubt it very much, based on the micro-level political participation and atti- tudes reported here and attitudes reported in other studies (Booth and Richard 2006; Booth and Seligson 1984; Booth and Seligson 2005; Booth, Wade, and Walker 2006). Because the poor are simply not authoritarian, it seems unlikely that participation of any sort by the poor would be politically destabilizing or have the capacity to usher in a wave of system-level authoritarianism driven by the preferences of the poor majority.

Finally, except for education, we have found little connection between systemic economic development or personal wealth and individual political participation in Latin America. Why is that so? In part, we believe that Lipset may have been wrong about the authoritarian potential of mass participation. Indeed, even if his claims were correct at the time of his study in the late 1950s, he is clearly wrong now. Why do we find such a discrepancy between the values and behaviors of Latin Americans as described by Lipset and those in our eight-nation study? One reason may be that mass behaviors and values have changed over time and circumstances between the era of Lipset's research when the region had few democracies and today when it has many elected, constitutional regimes. Indeed, only Costa Rica among our eight countries was democratic fifty years ago, but all the rest have joined the democratic club since the 1980s. It is thus possible that, even if Lipset was correct about wealth being linked to participation and democratic norms at the time he did his analysis, the subsequent diffusion of democratic rules of the game through the region may well have changed things. The new rules may have allowed or conditioned contemporary Latin Americans to participate more in politics and embrace democratic norms, irrespective of their wealth, than would have been true in the 1950s.

We do not have the tools or the data to account for the many questions raised by this striking difference between what Lipset hypothesized and today's observed political behavior and culture in Latin America. We do know, however, that in contemporary Latin American democracies poverty and wealth, personal or systemic, have remarkably little to do with participation and democratic values.

Appendix 4.A. Variables Used in the Study

Description of Indexes and Variables		Mean	St.Dev.
Independent Variables			
Socio-economic Inequality at the Individual Level			
Standard of living	An index constructed based on the respondent's report of possessing various articles of wealth: potable drinking water, indoor plumbing, television sets, refrigerator, cell phone, automobiles, washing machine, microwave oven, and computer (range 0–14).	4.95	3.35
Education	Total years of education completed	7.78	5.75
Socioeconomic Inequality at the Local and National Levels			
Size of community of residence	An ordinal measure of the relative population size/urbanization of the city/town/village in which the interview took place: national capital or metropolitan area (5), large city (4), medium city (3), small city (2), small town or rural area (1).	3.26	1.60
National wealth	Gross National Income, 2002, in U.S. dollars.	2,690.61	1,688.99
Welfare	Infant mortality per 1,000 live births, 2002.	25.62	8.73
Level of democracy	Vanhanen 1900–1989. Vanhanen Mean Democracy 1900–1989, scale 0–100. Vanhanen (1997).	3.79	2.05
Legitimacy Measures			
Existence of political community	To what degree are you proud to be a Costa Rican? (7-point scale, recoded into a great deal = 100, not at all = 0).		
	To what degree do you agree that in spite of our differences, we Costa Ricans have a lot of things and values that unite us as a country? (7-point scale, recoded into very much agree = 100, very much disagree = 0).	67.36	12.30

(continued)

Description of Indexes and Variables		Mean	St.Dev.
Support for core regime principles	I am going to read you a list of some actions or things that people can do to achieve their goals and political objectives. Please tell me to what degree do you approve or disapprove of people taking these actions: (10-point scale, 0 = strongly disapprove, 10 = strongly approve, transformed to a 0–100 range). That people participate in a legally permitted demonstration. That people participate in a group that tries to resolve community problems. That people work in an election campaign for a party or candidate.	67.66	18.48
Evaluation of regime performance	How would you rate, in general, the economic situation of the country? (5-point scale, recoded into very good = 100, very poor = 0). Do you think that over the next 12 months that the economic situation of the country will be better, the same or worse than it is now. (5-point scale, recoded into much better = 100, much worse = 0).	44.52	15.27
Support for regime institutions	All of the following are on a 7-point scale, 0 = none, 7 = much, transformed into 0–100). How much do you think the courts of Costa Rica guarantee a fair trial? How much do you respect the political institutions of Costa Rica? How much do you think citizens' basic rights are well protected by the Costa Rican political system? How proud do you feel to live under the Costa Rican political system? How much do you think one should support the Costa Rican political system?		

Description of Indexes and Variables		Mean	St.Dev.
	How much do you trust the Supreme Electoral Tribunal?		
	How much do you trust the Legislative Assembly?		
	How much do you trust the political parties?		
	How much do you trust the Supreme Court?	50.73	17.06
Support for local government	How much trust do you have in the municipality? (7-point scale, 0 = none, 100 = much).		
	Would you say that the services that the municipality is providing the people of your canton (county) are very good (100), good (75), neither good nor bad (50), bad (25), very bad (0)?		
	To what degree do the municipal officials pay attention to the people's wishes in meetings? A lot (100), somewhat (66), little (33), not at all (0)?		
	If you had a complaint about some local problem, and you took it to a member of the municipal council, how much attention would they pay you? A lot (100), somewhat (66), little (33), not at all (0)?	45.58	17.40
Support for political actors	All on a 7-point scale (nothing = 0, much = 100).		
	Referring to the incumbent government, how much did that government:		
	Fight poverty?		
	Combat government corruption?		
	Promote democratic principles?	48.80	23.18
Dependent Variables: Modes of Political Participation			
Voting	The respondent reported voting in immediate past presidential election (scored no = 0, yes = 1); and being registered to vote (scored no = 0, registration in process = .5, and registered = 1). These items are combined additively to yield an variable with a range of 0–2.	1.64	.61

Description of Indexes and Variables		Mean	St.Dev.
Contacting public officials	The respondent reported having contacted or not contacted each of three types of public officials: a legislator, ministry official, or local government official (no = 0, yes = 1 for each; range 0–3).	.16	.27
Communal activism	Respondent reported helping to solve a community problem within the last year, as well as donating money, contributing work, attending meetings, and organizing a new group to solve a problem.		
	(Respondent receives 1 point for responding affirmatively to each item; range = 0–5).	1.10	1.69

5

The Poor and the Viability of Democracy

Adam Przeworski

Introduction

This chapter begins where others have ended, namely, with the finding that poor people differ little in their attitudes toward democracy, their political values, and in the actual rates of electoral participation from those who are better off. Even if they may be more likely to see democracy in instrumental terms, the poor value democracy and participate in democratic politics. What do these facts imply for the viability of democracy?[1]

How could the poor threaten democracy? We need to distinguish three possibilities:

First, by not participating. Democracy is anemic and vulnerable when participation is low. Indeed, we commonly read low rates of turnout as indications of a crisis of democracy, as weakness of "diffuse support" (Easton 1968) for democratic institutions. The causal mechanism typically entailed here is that when the poor do not participate, they may end up exploding in the form of peasant revolts, ghetto riots, millenarian movements, and so on.

Second, by participating while being vulnerable to authoritarian appeals. The prototype of this scenario was the 1851 plebiscite in France, in which poor peasants supported the coup of Louis Napoleon. The specter that haunted American political science during the cold

---

[1] This section draws on Przeworski (2005) as well as Benhabib and Przeworski (2006).

war was that when the masses of the poor become politicized, they are vulnerable to extremist, read communist, appeals. This was the great fear of participation in the 1960s (Almond 1954; Huntington 1968; Shils 1965).

Third, by participating and being vulnerable to redistributive appeals. I distinguish this mechanism from the previous one, because here the poor are deeply committed to democracy, which they see as instrumental for their interests, but they frighten the wealthy, who turn to authoritarianism for protection. This was Marx's (1850, 1851) interpretation of the 18th Brumaire of Luis Napoleon.

All these are rather rough stories. My point is only that the macro consequences of the micro evidence presented in this volume are not obvious. Note that in the first story democracy is unstable when the poor do not participate; in the second story, democracy is unstable when they participate without being committed to democracy; in the last story, it is unstable when they participate and are committed to democracy. As I read the other chapters, I see that the poor participate, are committed to democracy, but also want democracy to improve their lives. So perhaps the issue of the stability of democracy hinges on the reactions of the wealthy to the democratically processed demands of the poor? This is, indeed, what I argue in the following: Increased participation of the poor is a threat to democracy only in situations where elites, fearing drastic redistribution, are prone to overthrow democracy. For the poor themselves, democracy might be the only viable means to get what they want. Yet, if they act precipitously, they may lose even that chance.

Macro–Micro Issues

Because several chapters in this volume invoke Lipset, his views are a natural place from which to depart. In several passages, Lipset (1960) maintained that poor people are unprepared for democracy or ill-disposed to obey democratic norms: the poor are more likely to succumb to appeals of irresponsible demagogues, they are rigid and intolerant and authoritarian, easily attracted to extremist movements. Political participation by the poor is thus a threat to democracy.

Additionally, if the distribution of incomes does not become more unequal as average income increases, then in countries with lower per capita income there are relatively more poor people. Hence, democracy is more fragile in poorer countries.

Lipset's description of political attitudes of poor people finds no support in the evidence presented in this volume. But suppose that he were correct: Would the conclusion follow? The issue is methodological. Before proceeding, therefore, it is necessary to dispel any notion that the stability of democracy can be inferred from individual attitudes, values, norms, or what not.

The idea that the viability of democracy can be read from individual attitudes was introduced into political science by Almond and Verba (1963), who also ushered in a new methodology. Almond and Verba claimed that while technological aspects of the Western culture were easy to diffuse to the new nations, Western political culture was less transmittable. There is a causal relation between culture and democracy: "If the democratic model of the participatory state is to develop in these new nations, it will require more than the formal institutions of democracy.... A democratic form of participatory political system requires as well a political culture consistent with it" (1963: 3). Although Almond and Verba accepted that economic development is necessary for democracy, they claimed it was not sufficient, as evidenced by the fact that the correlations found by Lipset were far from perfect. For Almond and Verba, culture furnishes the "psychological basis" of democracy. Moreover, as distinct from Laswell (1946) and other studies in the psychoanalytic vein, theirs was a mentalistic psychology. Culture is the "psychological orientation toward social objects.... When we speak of the political culture," Almond and Verba explained, "we refer to the political system as internalized in the cognition, feelings, and evaluations of its population." And finally, "The political culture of a nation is the particular distribution of patterns of orientation toward political objects among the members of the nation" (1963: 13). Given this conceptualization, culture can be studied by asking questions of individuals. The culture of a nation is nothing but a distribution of the answers. Their methodological innovation was thus to replace what used to be studied as "the national character" by examining history or as "the modal personality" by inquiring into patterns of child-rearing with answers to questions about what individuals knew, liked, and valued.

The culture Almond and Verba identified as democratic, "the civic culture," bore an uncanny resemblance to what one would expect to find in the United States, so it was not surprising that the United States best fit the ideal of democratic culture, followed by Great Britain. Because democracy in these countries was older – more stable – than in Germany, Italy, or Mexico, their central hypothesis withstood the test of evidence: a particular kind of political culture is required for a stable democracy. Inglehart (1990) and Granato, Inglehart, and Leblang (1996) attempted to validate this approach. Inglehart's (1990) "civil culture" consists of three indicators: (1) interpersonal trust, (2) life satisfaction, and (3) support for revolutionary change (which is expected to be detrimental to democracy). He and his collaborators found that these variables, when taken together, are statistically related to the number of continuous years of democracy between 1900 and 1980 and between 1920 and 1995 in a sample of twenty-four countries. Yet doubts remained (Jackman and Miller 1996): (1) Is this an appropriate measure of democratic stability? (2) Can one draw such inferences on the basis of a sample heavily biased in favor of long-lasting democracies? (3) What is the direction of causality? Muller and Seligson (1994) reanalyzed Inglehart's data, adding some Latin American countries, to identify the direction of causality. They concluded that, if anything, it is democratic stability that breeds the democratic culture, rather than vice versa.

Asking people questions about their attitudes toward democracy is now a huge industry all around the world. Answers to these questions are interpreted as "barometers" of democratic stability and are read nervously. Brazil, for example, seemed to verge on the brink in 1991 when only 39 percent of the respondents thought that democracy is always the best system of government, as contrasted with, say, Chile, in 1990 where 76 percent did. Yet these answers do not predict whether democracy survives or falls.

Given all we know about the viability of democracy, the idea that it stands or falls on any aggregation of individual attitudes appears strange. It is enough to consult any analysis of democratic breakdowns, from the seminal work of Linz and Stepan (1978), to Abraham's (1987) analysis of Weimar, Figueiredo's (1993) study of Brazil, or Schwartzman's (1980) research on the first democratic republic in Portugal, to discover the relevance of economic structures, of interests of economic groups, of postures of the military, and of institutional frameworks. If the viability of democracy hinges on anything, the first place to look are the strategies of those political forces that have the capacity to overthrow it. These strategies, in turn, depend on the structure interests, on the distribution of military force, and on the institutional arrangements.

If the fragility of democracies in poor countries is not the result of the individual attitudes of the poor, why are democracies less viable in poorer societies? One does not need to reach beyond Lipset to find an alternative explanation:

The general income level of a nation also affects its receptivity to democratic norms. If there is enough wealth in the country so that it does not make too much difference whether some redistribution takes place, it is easier to accept the idea that it does not matter greatly which side is in power. But if loss of office means serious losses for major groups, they will seek to retain office by any means available. (1960: 51)

Here the poor are no longer the culprit. The actors are "major groups" and what threatens democracy are distributional conflicts. If democracy is more fragile in poor countries, it is because conflicts over distribution are sharper when there is less to distribute. When threatened with redistribution, major groups defend themselves by any means they have at their disposal, and military force must be obviously among them.

Here are some stories. There was an election in Costa Rica in 1948, when that country had per capita income of about $1,500. The election was technically tied: the two candidates received almost the same number of votes, and there were widespread allegations of fraud, so that it was impossible to determine who, in fact, won. It was not clear who should decide, but the Congress took it upon itself to declare as the winner the candidate who officially received somewhat fewer votes. A civil war ensued, in which about 3,000 people were killed. At another time, there was an election in another country. The election was technically tied: the two candidates received almost the same number of votes, and there were widespread allegations of fraud, so that it was impossible to determine who, in fact, won. It was not clear who should decide, but the Supreme Court, appointed in part by one of the candidates' father, took it upon itself to declare as the winner the candidate who officially received somewhat fewer votes. Then everyone drove home in their SUVs to cultivate their gardens. They had SUVs and gardens because this country has per capita income of about $20,000. Whatever the reason for compliance, these facts tell us that political forces obey the results of the democratic process if the country is rich, whereas they may or may not if it is poor. And the difference is – this time Lipset had it right – that in poorer countries more is at stake.

Income and the Survival of Democracy: Some Facts

Lipset (1960) noticed that most economically developed countries had democratic regimes, while few poor countries did. Przeworski and Limongi (1997), in turn, have shown that this cross-sectional pattern is due to a different effect of per capita incomes on the survival of democracies and autocracies. Specifically, with the remarkable exception of India, democracies have been fragile in poor countries, while they are perfectly resilient in wealthy ones. The numbers are eloquent. Between 1950 and 1999, the probability that a democracy would die during any year in countries with per capita income less than $1,000 (1985 ppp dollars) was 0.0845, so that one in twelve democracies died. In countries with incomes between $1,001 and $3,000, this probability was 0.0362, for one in twenty-eight. Between $3,001 and $6,055, this probability was 0.0163, one in sixty-one. And no democracy ever fell in a country with per capita income more than that of Argentina in 1975, $6,055. This is a startling fact, given that throughout history about seventy democracies collapsed in poorer countries, while thirty-seven democracies spent over 1000 years in more developed countries and not one died. A picture tells it all: Figure 5.1 shows the probability of democracies dying as a function of per capita income (measured in 1996 purchasing power parity dollars).

But is income not a proxy for something else? Table 5.1 shows probit regressions in which the dependent variable are deaths of

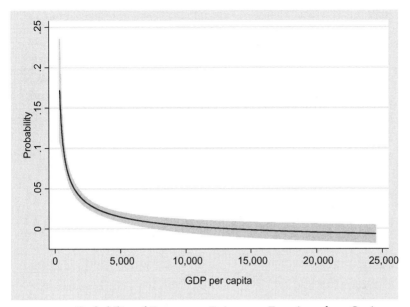

FIGURE 5.1. Probability of Democracy Dying, as a Function of per Capita Income.

democracies and the column headings specify the rival hypotheses. The most obvious candidate for a rival explanation is education. Taking the years of education of an average member of the labor force (from Bhalla 1994), one learns that education plays some additional role in sustaining democracy, but it does not reduce the importance of income. Coser (1956) argued, and many sociologists following him agreed, that democracy is easier to sustain if a country has a complex social structure. Coser's argument was that when social structure is complex, cleavages overlap, rather than pit one large group against another. (See also Ross 1960.) This argument is tested by calculating labor force fractionalization, that is, the probability that two random members of the labor force do not work in the same of nine one-digit sectors (this variable is called *complexity*, from Kim 2004). Complexity strongly reduces the probability that a democracy would die, but income still matters. John Stuart Mill (1991: 230) had argued already in 1860 that democracy is more difficult to sustain in countries ridden with ethno-linguistic divisions. With all the caveats about measuring

TABLE 5.1. *Transitions to Dictatorship as a Function of Per Capita Income and Rival Variables*

	None	Education	Complexity	ELF*	Inequality
Constant	−1.3066	−0.7771	−2.5750	−1.0137	−0.8037
	(0.1161)	(0.2002)	(1.1970)	(0.1528)	(0.6409)
GDP/cap	−0.2262	−0.1820	−0.1959	−0.1755	−0.2734
	(0.0426)	(0.0633)	(0.1103)	(0.0404)	(0.0867)
Rival		−0.0816	−5.5095	−0.6373	−0.0050
		(0.0504)	(1.7709)	(0.2518)	(0.0140)
N**	2423	1085	1201	2234	771
TDA***	47	30	10	46	14

Note: Standard errors in parentheses.
* ELF is Ethno-Linguistic Fractionalization. ** N is the number of observations. *** TDA is the number of transitions to autocracy in the particular sample.

ethnicity across cultures, using the index of ethno-linguistic fractional-ization, ELF60 (from Easterly and Levine 1997) shows that although democracies are less likely to die in the more homogeneous countries, the role of income continues to be important. Finally, democracy may be more fragile in more unequal societies. Because the data on inequal-ity are scarce, unreliable, and not easily compared across countries, all we can do is to take the high quality data from Deininger and Squire (1996) and extend them by attributing the same degree of inequality to two years before and after each observation. The resulting sample is still heavily biased in favor of wealthy countries, an additional reason to take the results with a grain of salt. With all these caveats, income distribution appears not to matter in regression, whereas income con-tinues to do so. When, however, the observations of inequality are dichotomized by GINI = 0.35, the odds of democracy falling are 4.7 higher in the more unequal countries. The difference is even more pronounced when the observations are dichotomized by $Q_1/Q_5 = 9$, because no democracy fell in the cases more equal by this criterion. Hence, there are reasons to suspect that democracy is more brittle in unequal societies. Yet, in the end, although other factors do matter, none of the rival hypotheses for which data exist eliminates the role of income.

Why Does Average Income Matter?

To approach this question, ask first what redistributions of income and assets are feasible in a democracy, given the initial assets, their distribution, and some features of the political environment. The question is motivated by the possibility that if the redistribution is either insufficient for the poor or excessive for the wealthy, they may turn against democracy. Moreover, if no redistribution simultaneously satisfies the poor and the wealthy and if either group has any chance to establish its dictatorship, democracy cannot be sustained.

Without getting mired in definitional discussions, here is how democracy works: (for a fuller account, see Przeworski 1991, chapter 1):

(1) Interests or values are in conflict. If they were not, if interests were harmonious or values were unanimously shared, anyone's decisions would be accepted by all, so that anyone could be a benevolent dictator.

(2) The authorization to rule is derived from elections.

(3) Elections designate "winners" and "losers." This designation is an instruction to the participants as to what they should and should not do. Democracy is in equilibrium when winners and losers obey the instructions inherent in their designations.

(4) Democracy functions under a system of rules. Some rules, notably those that map the results of elections on the designations of winners and losers, say the majority rule, are "constitutive" in the sense of Searle (1995), that is, they enable behaviors that would not be possible without them. But most rules emerge in equilibrium: they are but descriptions of equilibrium strategies.

Democracy endures only if it self-enforcing. It is not a contract because there are no third parties to enforce it. To survive, democracy must be an equilibrium at least for those political forces that can overthrow it: given that others respect democracy, each must prefer it over the feasible alternatives. And it is an equilibrium as long as these forces obey the results of the democratic process, accepting the costs associated with these results.

An analysis of these assumptions generates the following conclusions. Conditional on the initial income distribution and the capacity of the poor and the wealthy to overthrow democracy, each country has a threshold of wealth above which democracy survives. This threshold is lower when the distribution of initial endowments is more equal and when the military prowess of these groups is lower. In the extreme, democracy survives at any income if its distribution is sufficiently egalitarian or if neither group can establish dictatorship. Yet, in poor unequal countries there exists no redistribution scheme that would be accepted both by the poor and the wealthy. Hence, democracy cannot survive. As endowments increase, redistribution schemes that satisfy both the poor and the wealthy emerge. Moreover, as average wealth grows, the wealthy tolerate more and the poor less redistribution, so that the set of feasible redistributions becomes larger. Because the median voter prefers one such scheme to the dictatorship of either group, the outcome of electoral competition is obeyed by everyone and democracy survives.

These results are driven by an assumption about preferences. The cost of dictatorship is the loss of freedom. People suffer disutility when they are not free to live the lives of their choosing (Sen 1991). This preference against dictatorship (or for democracy) is independent of income: as Dasgupta (1993: 47) put it, the view that the poor do not care about freedoms associated with democracy "is a piece of insolence that only those who don't suffer from their lack seem to entertain" (see also Sen 1994). Yet, because the marginal utility of income declines as income increases, while the dislike of dictatorship is independent of income, at a sufficiently high income the additional gain that would accrue from being able to dictate tax rates becomes too small to overcome the loss of freedom.

Figure 5.2 illustrates redistributions that are acceptable to the wealthy (all below the upper line) and the poor (all above the lower line) when both groups have equal military power and the distribution of income is moderately unequal. As we see, when per capita income (y, measured in multiples of $250) is low, no redistribution satisfies the wealthy and the poor simultaneously. In turn, when income is high, the rich accept a higher degree of redistribution, whereas the poor are satisfied with a lower degree. Hence, democracy cannot survive in such societies if they are poor, but it can when they are wealthy.

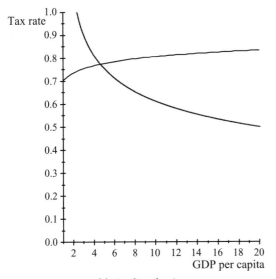

FIGURE 5.2. Feasible Redistributions.

Clearly, this entire story is highly schematic. My only point is that the average income of a country may matter for the viability of democracy not because the poor value democracy less but because the rich are more afraid of demands for redistribution and are more prone to defend their power by any means. To put it in a nutshell, the poor are more of a threat to the interests of the rich in poorer societies.

From Representative Institutions to Democracy

The very pairing of "Poor People and Democracy," the title of this volume, could appear on the intellectual horizon only quite recently, basically during the second half on the past century. When first established – in England, the United States, France, Spain, and the newly independent Latin American republics – representative government was not a "democracy" as we would now define the term, nor was it seen as such by its founders (Dunn 2004; Manin 1997). In spite of their egalitarian pronouncements, the problem of "founders," pretty much everywhere, was how to construct representative government for the propertied while protecting it from the poor. As a result, political rights were everywhere restricted to wealthy males.

Although some early constitutions made male suffrage nearly universal, during most of the nineteenth century the right to vote was confined to adult men who owned property, earned some amount of income, or paid some amount of taxes. Except for a few landowners in the Austrian Empire, no women could vote in national elections before 1893. These original restrictions were either gradually or abruptly relaxed as time went on. Yet, the road from representative government to democracy took a long time to traverse. As of 1900, one country had fully universal suffrage, whereas seventeen enfranchised all males. Only during the second half of the twentieth century, more than 150 years after representative institutions were first established, did poor people gain full political rights.

The fear of the political participation by the poor was widespread. One need not impute motivations: it is sufficient to listen to the voices of the historical protagonists. A Connecticut representative, Samuel Dana, thought in 1789 that it was quite proper that the society would be divided into "the rich, the few, the rulers" and "the poor, the many, the ruled" (cited in Dunn 2004: 23). The drafter of the French Constitution of 1795, Boissy d'Anglas, declared that "We must be ruled by the best... a country governed by property-owners is within the social order, that which is dominated by non-property owners is in a state of nature" (cited in Crook 1996: 46). The consensus in mid-nineteenth century Colombia was that "We want enlightened democracy, a democracy in which intelligence and property direct the destinies of the people; we do not want a barbarian democracy in which the proletarianism and ignorance drown the seeds of happiness and bring the society to confusion and disorder" (Gutiérrez Sanin 2003: 185). "The right to make laws belongs to the most intelligent, to the aristocracy of knowledge, created by nature," a Peruvian constitutionalist, Bartolomé Herrera, declared in 1846 (Sobrevilla 2002: 196); the Peruvian theorist José María Pando maintained that "a perpetual aristocracy... is an imperative necessity"; the Chilean Andrés Bello wanted rulers to constitute "a body of wise men (un cuerpo de sabios)"; whereas the Spanish conservative thinker Donoso Cortés juxtaposed the sovereignty of the wise to sovereignty of the people (Gargarella 2005: 120). Still by 1867, Walter Bagehot (1963: 277) would warn that:

It must be remembered that a political combination of the lower classes, as such and for their own objects, is an evil of the first magnitude; that a permanent combination of them would make them (now that many of them have the suffrage) supreme in the country; and that their supremacy, in the state they now are, means the supremacy of ignorance over instruction and of numbers over knowledge.

Although the prevalence of *suffrage censitaire* may appear to contradict the norm of suppressing all distinctions in society and to be incompatible with the principle of political equality, suffrage restrictions were portrayed by their proponents as serving the common good of all. The French Declaration of Rights qualified its recognition of equality in the sentence that immediately followed: "Men are born equal and remain free and equal in rights. Social distinctions may be founded only upon the general good." The argument for restricting suffrage was spelled out already by Montesquieu (1748/1995: 155), who parted from the principle that "All inequality under democracy should be derived from the nature of democracy and from the very principle of democracy." His example was that people who must continually work to live are not prepared for public office or would have to neglect their functions. As barristers of Paris put it on the eve of the Revolution, "Whatever respect one might wish to show for the rights of humanity in general, there is no denying the existence of a class of men who, by virtue of their education and the type of work to which their poverty had condemned them, is ... incapable at the moment of participating fully in public affairs" (cited in Crook 1996: 13). "In such cases," Montesquieu went on, "equality among citizens can be lifted in a democracy for the good of democracy. But it is only apparent equality which is lifted ..." The generic argument, to be found in slightly different versions, was that: (1) Representation is acting in the best interest of all. (2) To determine the best interest of all one needs reason. (3) Reason has sociological determinants: not having to work for a living ("disinterest"), or not being employed or otherwise dependent on others ("independence"). As a Chilean statesman put it in 1865, to exercise political rights it is necessary "to have the intelligence to recognize the truth and the good, the will to want it, and the freedom to execute it." (A speech by Senador Abdón Cifuentes, cited in Maza Valenzuela 1995: 153). In turn, the claim that only apparent equality is being violated was built in three steps: (1) Acting in the best common interest considers everyone equally, so that everyone is equally represented. (2) The only quality that is being distinguished is the capacity to recognize the common good. (3) No one is barred from acquiring this quality, so that suffrage is potentially open to all.

The self-serving nature of these convoluted arguments for restricting suffrage was apparent. A French conservative polemicist, J. Mallet du Pan, was perhaps first to insist in 1796 that legal equality must lead to equality of wealth: "Do you wish a republic of equals amid the inequalities which the public services, inheritances, marriage, industry and commerce have introduced into society? You will have to overthrow property" (cited by Palmer 1964: 230).[2] Madison, who in Federalist #10 maintained that representative government would protect property, was less sanguine some decades later: "the danger to the holders of property can not be disguised, if they are undefended against a majority without property. Bodies of men are not less swayed by interest than individuals.... Hence, the liability of the rights of property...." (Note written at some time between 1821 and 1829, in Ketcham 1986: 152). The Scottish philosopher James Mackintosh predicted in 1818 that if the "laborious classes" gain franchise, "a permanent animosity between opinion and property must be the consequence" (Cited in Collini, Winch, and Burrow, 1983: 98). David Ricardo was prepared to extend suffrage only "to that part of them which cannot be supposed to have an interest in overturning the right to property" (In Collini et al., 1983: 107). Thomas Macaulay (1900: 263) in the 1842 speech on the Chartists vividly summarized the danger presented by universal suffrage:

The essence of the Charter is universal suffrage. If you withhold that, it matters not very much what else you grant. If you grant that, it matters not at all what else you withhold. If you grant that, the country is lost.... My firm conviction is that, in our country, universal suffrage is incompatible, not only

---

[2] Hamilton formulated something like this syllogism in his "Plan for the National Government" (in Ketcham 1986: 75), delivered at the Convention on June 18, 1796: "In every community where industry is encouraged, there will be a division of it into the few and the many. Hence separate interests will arise. There will be debtors and creditors, etc. Give all power to the many, they will oppress the few." Yet, he thought, like Madison, that this effect can be prevented.

with this or that form of government, and with everything for the sake of which government exists; that it is incompatible with property and that it is consequently incompatible with civilization.

Systems of representative government were thus born under a mortal fear that participation by the broad masses of the population, a large part of whom were poor and illiterate, would threaten property. Suffrage was a dangerous weapon. Yet, the poor did not think that their best interests were being represented by the propertied, and they would struggle for suffrage. The elites resisted as long as they could and yielded only when they could not.

Suffrage, Turnout, and Electoral Participation

Examining the evolution of electoral participation over the long run shows that almost the entire increase in participation was due to the progressive enfranchisement of the new groups, rather than to changes of turnout among those who had the right to vote. Note that defining electoral participation as the ratio of actual voters to the population,[3] we can decompose it by the following tautology:

$$\frac{\text{voters}}{\text{population}} = \frac{\text{eligibles}}{\text{population}} \times \frac{\text{voters}}{\text{eligibles}}$$

where the entire tautology is conditional on an election occurring at all. *Participation* is then the ratio of voters to the population, *eligibility* is the ratio of the number of people legally qualified to vote to the population, whereas *turnout* is the ratio of actual voters to the eligible voters. In this language,

participation = eligibility * turnout.

With these definitions, we can decompose the rise of political participation into a part that is due to changes in eligibility and a part that is due to changes of turnout. The purpose of this accounting exercise is to weigh those changes in participation that were voluntary, at least insofar as individuals had the legal right to decide whether or not to

---

[3] Using the total population as the base introduces a bias that is due to the ageing of the population. Data on age composition, however, are scarce.

vote, against those changes that resulted from extensions of political rights.

During the entire period between 1800 to the present, participation increased on the average by 1.33 percentage points between any two successive elections for which data are available.[4] Eligibility increased by 1.89, whereas the turnout of the eligible increased by only 0.17. Decomposing the change in participation shows that the average increase in participation was due exclusively to increases in eligibility: of the average increase in participation, 1.33, 1.36 is due to eligibility and 0.03 to turnout.[5] One should not infer from these numbers, however, that the evolution of eligibility has been smooth. When the electorate was expanding, it was typically in spurts resulting from extensions of suffrage. Eligibility jumped on the average by 16.8 percentage points in the fifty-four cases when suffrage restrictions were relaxed, and it drifted upward by only 1.3 points when suffrage rules remained the same.[6] Turnout of those eligible increased on the average by 5.0 points in the first elections under expanded suffrage. Decomposing the increase of participation immediately following the extension of suffrage, 13.9 percentage points, shows again that most of this increase was due to increased eligibility. Hence, legal provisions regulating the right to vote were much more important in determining whether participation increased than individual choices.

---

[4] Note that in some cases information about intervening elections is not available. Moreover, the periods covered may span episodes during which the government was not elected.

[5] Mathematically, let P stand for participation, E for eligibility, T for turnout, and Δ for forward change between two successive elections. Since, $P_t = E_t T_t$, $\Delta P_t = \Delta E_t * T_t + E_t * \Delta T_t + \Delta E_t * \Delta T_t$ or, $\Delta P_t = T_t * \Delta E_t + \Delta T_t * E_{t+1}$. The first product on the right-hand side is the part that is due to increases in eligibility, the second to increases of turnout.

[6] The drift was due to increasing real incomes, inflation, or increasing literacy. For example, the annual income requirement in Imperial Brazil was 100 milreis in 1824, raised to 200 in 1846, and Graham (2003: 360) reports that because of inflation everyone except for beggars and vagabonds, even servants, earned enough to satisfy this criterion. As Seymour (1915) pointed out, the crucial consequences of the British reform of 1832 was not that it enfranchised many new voters but that it opened a possibility of gaining political rights by acquiring wealth, and Plumb (1973) claims that the English 40-shilling requirement lost its restrictive effect by the early eighteenth century because of inflation.

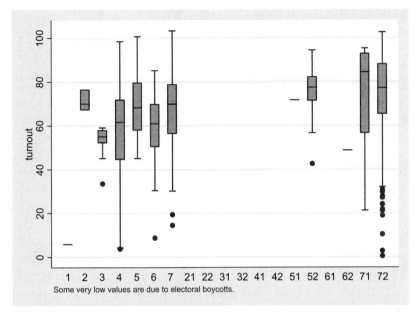

FIGURE 5.3. Turnout by Suffrage Qualifications. Coding of suffrage qualifications: For males: 2 property; 3 income and literacy; 4 income; 5 literacy or
(income or literacy); 6 "independent"; 7 universal. For females: first digit gives
qualifications for males; second digit = 1 indicates that women had to satisfy
stricter requirements; second digit = 2 indicates that they qualified on the same
basis as males.

As long as franchise was restricted, the poor simply could not vote.
Combining information about suffrage with data on turnout, we can
read Figure 5.3 as saying that when suffrage was conditioned on property, voters were comprised of one-half of male property owners and
no one else. In turn, when suffrage was restricted to literate males,
voters were comprised of about 60 percent of literates.

Once suffrage became broad, however, it is not possible to tell
who voted and who did not without information from micro-level
data. Although not exactly the same, however, such data are now
available for a wide range of countries. This information adds up to
the conclusion that people who are relatively poorer, whether in terms
of income or some other understanding of poverty, are not less likely
to vote than those who are better off. Recalculating the data reported

by Anduiza (1999: 102) for fourteen Western European countries shows that the average difference between the turnout of the top and bottom income quartiles was only 6 percent. The largest difference, in France, was 16.4 percent. According to Norris' (2002: 93–4) analysis of pooled data from twenty-two countries, the difference in turnout between the highest and the lowest quantile was 9.6, but this sample includes the United States. Norris' (2004: 174) data for thirty-one countries in 1996, including again the United States, shows this difference to be 8 percent. Moving outside Europe and its wealthy offshoots to poorer countries shows again that income has no impact on turnout. Yadav (1999) found that members of the scheduled castes and registered tribes voted at higher rates than people who were better off in India during the 1990s; a finding confirmed by Krishna (in this volume) within north Indian villages. Using data from Afrobarometer for fifteen African countries, Bratton (in this volume) found that the poor were somewhat more likely to vote than the non-poor. Booth and Seligson (in this volume) report that in a pooled analysis of six Central American countries plus Mexico and Colombia turnout was not related to income.[7] But there is a clear outlier to these results: according to Verba et al. (1995: 190), in the United States, 86 percent of those with incomes of $75,000 or more turned out at the polls, only one-half of those with incomes less than $15,000 did.

The impact of education seems to vary more across countries. Bratton (in this volume) as well as Booth and Seligson (in this volume) find that educated people are somewhat more likely to vote in their respective regions. Norris (2002: 93–4) estimates the difference of turnout between college graduates and high school dropout to be 9.5 percent, whereas her sample of thirty-one countries in 1996 shows a difference of 14 percent (2004: 175). Yet Norris emphasizes that education has no effect on turnout in Western Europe. Anduiza's (1999: 99) data show the difference between the turnout of "high" and "low" levels of education to be only 2.3 percent in fifteen European countries, with

---

[7] Gaviria, Panizza, and Seddon (2002: 5) report that in seventeen Latin American countries, "participation (in a broader sense) is surprisingly homogeneous across socioeconomic strata." They do not have data on turnout but concoct a scale of participation from attitudes toward politics.

six countries in which people with low levels of education turnout at higher rates than the most educated population. The greatest difference in favor of the highly educated population is in Switzerland, which is an outlier at 19.2 percent. Goodrich and Nagler (2006) data show the average difference between the top and bottom quartiles of education to be 8.3 percent in fifteen countries not including the United States, with Switzerland again the outlier at 22.7 percent. They also show the difference for the United States: it is 39.6 percent.

To summarize these findings differently, about 85 percent of people in the bottom income quartile vote in Western Europe (Anduiza 1999: 102), about 75 percent of people in the bottom quantile voted in twenty-two countries in Norris' (2002) sample, which is almost the same as in Norris' (2004) sample of thirty-one countries, both including the United States. About 88 percent of people with low levels of education vote in Western Europe (Anduiza 1999: 99), about 77 percent in Norris' sample of twenty-two countries, and about 68 percent in her sample of thirty-one countries, again including the United States. In the United States, about one-half of people with low income or low education levels do not vote.

I will not venture into explanations. Placing the United States in a cross-national context immediately points to the fact that it is one of the few countries, along with France, where registration is not automatic and before 1993 was quite difficult in most states. Delving into history shows that the introduction of various registration impediments at the end of the nineteenth century sharply reduced turnout, with a ballpark estimate of about one-third (Testi 1998). Yet, registration requirements were relaxed and made uniform in 1993 with some effect on registration but almost no effect on turnout (for a summary literature on this topic, see Hill 2006). Moreover, different estimates converge to the conclusion that even if registration were automatic, turnout in the United States would increase by no more than 10 percent, which would still leave it well below the rate of other countries. Hence, something other than registration is at play.

All I can conclude is that somehow in the United States the poor are successfully barred from electoral politics, in spite of universal suffrage, egalitarian ideology, and all the ostensible devotion to democracy. But my reason to highlight the United States was to show that it is not absolute income that shapes individual electoral participation. The people who are poor in the United States still have incomes higher than many who are relatively well-off in poor countries. Yet, they participate in voting at much lower rates.

Conclusions

Although I could not muster direct evidence, all these bits and pieces add up to the conclusion that the poor are a danger to democracy only to the extent that should the democratic process call for a significant redistribution of wealth, this would scare the rich, pushing them into the arms of those who control physical force. Instances in which a democracy fell to a left-wing dictatorship are extremely rare: Czechoslovakia in 1948, Peru in 1968, perhaps Venezuela at the present. Almost all left-wing dictatorships, of which there have been quite a few, followed dictatorships of the right. In turn, right-wing dictatorships arising as a response to popular clamor for redistribution are ubiquitous. Marx did exaggerate when he claimed that democracy is incompatible with capitalism: in several countries democracy and private ownership coexist peacefully. Yet, the story he told about the 1848–1851 period in France has been repeated over and over again.

Some facts are stark. Systems of representative government were born under a fear of participation by the broad masses of the population, a large part of who were poor and illiterate. One would not err much thinking that the strategic problem of "founders," pretty much everywhere, was how to construct representative government for the rich while protecting it from the poor. And even when the poor conquered the right to participate, in many instances a plethora of institutional devices muted their voice. As one speaker observed in the Spanish parliamentary debate about universal suffrage in 1889, "We are going to establish universal suffrage, and then what is going to happen in our national political history? Nothing... the Congress of Deputies will continue working as it is doing now; the legislative power will be wielded by the Crown with the Cortes; the Crown will have... all the guarantees and privileges given by the Constitution of 1876" (cited in Garrido 1998: 213). Or, as Graham (2003: 364) put it with regard to free Afro-Brazilians, "Their vote was allowed because the results could be manipulated." Because particular institutional devices affect the rich and the poor differentially,[8] they were often used to make the voice of the poor inaudible.

In countries where left-wing parties and trade unions succeeded in organizing the people who were poor, disciplined their distributional claims, won office, and intelligently managed the market economy, democratic institutions led to increasing prosperity and declining inequality. It was not obvious that extending political rights to the poor would be sufficient to mitigate their revolutionary ardor. Although from the moment of their formation, socialist parties demanded universal suffrage, for quite a long time they were ambivalent about how to use it. Yet, after years of heated discussions (about which see Przeworski 1986), Social Democrats became fully committed to electoral politics, even at the cost of economic sacrifices if these were necessary to defend democracy. As J. McGurk, the chairman of the Labour Party, put sharply in 1919

We are either constitutionalists or we are not constitutionalists. If we are constitutionalists, if we believe in the efficacy of the political weapon (and we are, or why do we have a Labour Party?) then it is both unwise and undemocratic because we fail to get a majority at the polls to turn around and demand that we should substitute industrial action. (cited in Miliband 1975: 69)

Not only did democracy survive, but it fulfilled the role poor people legitimately expect it should: to generate equality in the social and economic realms.

Yet, this feat has not been accomplished everywhere. In poor countries in which representative institutions coexist with flagrant economic and social inequality, populist appeals – anti-institutional, personalistic, demagogic, and often incoherent – do speak to the experience of poor people. In turn, those better off continue to defend their privileges, hiding behind the façade of democracy as long as it wills in their

---

[8] Anduiza (1999) offers the best discussion I have read of the impact of interactions between institutions and individual characteristics on voting.

favor but ready to defend them by other means if it would not. In such countries democracy remains fragile. But, as this volume amply demonstrates, it is not because the poor do not value democracy. Democracy is the best hope poor people have for improving their lives. If democracy is fragile in some countries, it is because this hope has not been fulfilled.

6

Conclusion

Implications for Policy and Research

Anirudh Krishna and John A. Booth

Since the mid-twentieth century academic and intellectual understandings of the role of mass publics in democracy has been Schumpeterian in its conclusion that extensive political participation by the poor or the working classes would be antithetical to democracy. This worldview arose from three major strains of research that informed and reinforced each other. One built on the rise of authoritarian politics in Europe between the first and second World Wars, a paradigm that attributed antidemocratic values to mass publics. Analysts concluded that should mass publics participate extensively in politics, authoritarian regimes would be the inevitable outcome, because the values and attitudes of poor people would foster such an outcome (Adorno et al. 1950; Lipset 1960, 1981; Schumpeter 1943). Later research on voting and citizen attitudes in the West concluded that working classes tended not to participate in politics as much as those of higher socioeconomic status (Almond and Verba 1963; Campbell et al. 1960; Milbraith 1965; Verba and Nie 1972; Verba, Nie, and Kim 1978). Third, research on the impact of development on regime type linked the emergence of democracy to economic modernization and prosperity (Almond and Verba 1963; Apter 1965; Lerner 1958). These findings combined into a worldview holding that the poor tend to hold authoritarian rather than democratic values; normally, they are rather politically inert. From these suppositions, it was deduced that only by reducing the political import of the poor – that is, by minimizing the political engagement of the poor while working, first, to increase the wealth of whole societies – democracy would be better assured of stability in the future. These findings and conclusions validated Schumpeter's misinterpretation of classical democratic theory by supporting the notion that elites must, at least initially, run a managed, controlled system and protect liberal institutions from dangerous, authoritarian masses.

The influence of this emerging understanding of class and political participation was enormous. For late-twentieth century political science, poor and working class citizens, in effect, became a hazard to liberal democracy. Bachrach (1966) and Pateman (1970) have shown that key empirical theorists took comfort in the supposedly scant participation of the poor.

The findings summarized in this volume contribute powerfully toward righting the view of mass publics in democracy. By rescuing the poor from their long-standing image as politically inert and/or authoritarian citizens, these findings help construct a more accurate depiction of facts on the ground. Independent data from Asia, Africa, and Latin America demonstrate that poor citizens in many developing countries are neither authoritarian nor politically inactive. This demonstration may allow more robust models of democratic governance in poor countries to be constructed and be better grounded in empirical fact. The denial of democracy on grounds of widespread poverty can be better exposed as what it is in practice: a ruse to obstruct and deny equality of political influence to the more numerous poor.

The received wisdom – empirically suspect findings now supplanted by better and more recent information from both the micro-political and macro-political level – has had it wrong. Other factors being equal, the poor in poor countries today embrace democracy and take part in politics as much as their more prosperous counterparts. Thus, the poor are not – and should not be – a reason for autocrats and coup leaders to justify their rule. The values and behaviors of poor people vis-à-vis democracy are not significantly different from the values and behaviors of richer people. Democracy is supported by the poor just as much as it is by the rich.

Education – rather than wealth – is what significantly enhances democratic engagement. Support for democracy and participation rates rise substantially when the veil of illiteracy is pulled back. Rapid increases in primary educational achievement in countries with low per capita GDP levels have helped generate widespread democratic engagement. Entirely unlettered people are not unintelligent by any means, but they are unable to consult as many information sources as those who can read. By providing them with a greater capacity to investigate, evaluate and compare alternatives, education helps people become more discerning consumers of democracy, much as classical democratic theory argued.

Those who wish to promote democracy would wisely invest in promoting education. Reducing illiteracy, by enhancing information and promoting self-esteem, will encourage more support for democracy and more democratic actions among mass publics. Such a strategy would likely strengthen democratic governance more directly and efficaciously than the myriad approaches now in vogue.

Democracy is not under threat from poor people just because they are poor (and therefore, as it was earlier presumed, less well acclimatized to democracy). But it can be under threat from a lack of institutionalized restraints.

Recent research strongly suggests that much of the original supposition attributing authoritarianism to poverty suffered from flaws. It does not bear up under more careful analysis (Altemeyer 1981, 1996, 2006; Dekker and Ester 1987, 1990; Martin 2001; Middendorp and Meloen 1990). Instead, to find evidence of authoritarian tendencies and support for authoritarian regimes, one must look not to the poorer sections but to the elites who control vital resources and political institutions. These elites often embrace frightening (but false) images of mass publics that serve narrow elite interests. Blaming mass publics for threatening democracy may thus be seen for what it is – a rationale used by elites for self-serving antidemocratic and exclusionary practice (Altemeyer 2004). New empirical evidence that overturns this false wisdom should – indeed must – allow and promote reconsideration of the real and potential roles of the poor in politics.

Scholars should begin to rehabilitate their understanding of the poor in politics and evaluate how true democracy might be promoted rather than avoided. This will require a break with the Schumpeterian world view, embraced and advanced by generations of Western political scientists, and a return to the classical understanding of democracy, combined with further solidly grounded research on the real values and participation of mass publics in developing nations.

For well over a century, the case was never made that democracy had economic pre-conditions and that its sustainability depended on economic growth and prosperity . . . the nineteenth-century demo-protection afforded by a liberal state did not have wealth requirements. To the extent that liberal democracy is conceived as a political form, a "poor democracy" is equally conceivable and possible. (Sartori 2001: 56)

The data presented in the preceding chapters amply demonstrate that these expectations have firm empirical micro-foundations.

Poor democracies, or democracies with large percentages of poor citizens, are not only conceivable; they have come into being in most parts of the world. Poor people are no less imbued than others with the values of democracy, and in many instances poor people partici-pate more actively than others in various acts associated with making democracy work.

The Only Game in Town?

Can democracy become the only game in town in countries inhab-ited by large numbers of people in poverty? Our expectation – tinged with more than a little hope – is that democracies may not be as easily reversed as they have been in the past. More widespread sup-port among an increasingly educated and better informed populace makes it harder for authoritarians to gain a firm footing (Altemeyer 2004; Dekker and Ester 1990; Fung and Wright 2001; Middendorp and Meloen 1990). A stronger and more globalized normative basis for democracy simultaneously makes it less likely that outside pow-ers will as readily support non-democracies abroad. Still, dangers to democracy remain.

Lack of institutionalized restraints of both normative and structural kinds makes it politically expedient sometimes for groups of elites to overturn democracy. Fears of authoritarian or military takeovers are reinforced by recent experiences, for example, in Bangladesh and Thailand. Elite takeovers are more likely, as Przeworki remarks (in this volume), in poorer countries where the level of inequality is also high. Democratically negotiated proposals may not suffice to resolve distributional disagreements, and elites commanding crucial political (and economic) resources may find it worth their while to fund and support a coup d'etat. Such situations are most likely to arise as a response to prior antidemocratic mobilization among the poor.

Channeling poor people's demands through the discipline of social democratic parties has enabled more gradual redistribution without democratic rupture in parts of Western Europe. Institutional innovation and investment are similarly critical for developing country democracies. For democracy to become more firmly consolidated within poorer countries institution building needs to be persisted with all seriousness.

An important aspect of such institutional innovation will need to be concerned with making democracy more democratic. Far from being a luxury good, one that is appreciated and enjoyed by richer more than poorer people, democracy is an aspiration equally of people possessing different levels of wealth. Indeed, for poorer people democracy often provides the only viable means of seeking justice and opportunity on an everyday basis. Richer people can have their purposes served through myriad avenues, including privileged access to decision makers, bribery, and corruption (You and Khagram 2005), but a poorer person must normally rely on how institutions routinely work. It is quite likely for this reason that poorer people, once they have been exposed to democracy and become familiar with its working, support it strongly and engage with it in the high numbers reported in this volume. Democracy is the best hope for improving the lives poor people have, Przeworki concludes (in this volume); if democracy is fragile in some countries, it is because this hope has not been fulfilled.

For the democratic expectations of the poor to be met fully or in large part, it is critical that the institutions of democracy must begin to function better. Democracy must not only exist and be made stronger; it must also become more democratic in terms of the protections, opportunities, and benefits routinely available to poorer citizens.[1]

---

[1] A substantial literature has developed around the idea of deepening democracy; a useful overview with case studies include Fung and Wright (2003).

Democratic channels must be accessible to all, with easily understood rules and processes and officials who can be held to account through low-cost and well-regarded means. Faith must become widespread that only through these channels are grievances and proposals legitimately routed. For democracy to survive and grow strong in this milieu, it is not sufficient that governments are elected democratically. The everyday practices of governance also need to become more democratic.

Attention is required to building democratic institutions, not only at the national level but also at intermediate and grassroots levels. Parliaments, parties, and the press are very important nationally, and strengthening these institutions is a critical part of the effort to sustain democracy. But these are not the places where the poor most often experience democracy in their everyday lives. Much more attention needs to be paid to building *middle-level institutions*. These are the institutions that can facilitate – but at present mostly hinder and constrain – ordinary citizens' everyday access to democratic rights and democratic remedies.

Political parties, local governments, NGOs, and other civil society organizations – institutions that, for want of a better term, we refer to collectively as mediating or "middle-level" institutions – are often weak to virtually nonexistent, especially in rural areas of developing countries, where large parts of the poorer populations reside. Under such circumstances, citizens are considerably handicapped in terms of access and information. A common theme in new democracies relates to significant institutional gaps in the middle that limit individuals' access to democratic protections and opportunities (Chabal and Daloz 1999; Chatterjee 2004; Friedman 2002; Vilas 1997). Lacking available institutional venues, communities can rarely hold public officials to account on a day-to-day basis, and individuals cannot easily complain when their democratic rights are violated by officials and others.

For most people in India, for example, the state is distant in both physical and cognitive terms.[2] A British colonial administrator, writing at the dawn of the twentieth century, before the advent of national

---

[2] In sub-Saharan Africa similarly, the state "has been left suspended in mid-air," aloof and afar from the majority of citizens (Hyden 1983: 195).

independence and of democracy, described the situation prevailing in India at that time.

> In England, justice goes to the people; in India, the people come to justice.... An aggrieved person might have to travel any distance up to fifty miles over a road-less country....A police matter, again, involved a journey to the station, perhaps ten miles off. Trials...involved much hanging about, many journeys to and fro, and a constant spending of money...[the villager] had to find his way to this strange tribunal in an unknown land as best he could, in charge of the police, whose tender mercies he dreaded, or alone. (Carstairs 1912: 12–3)

Significant changes have occurred since that distant time. In particular, governments at the national and state levels are now regularly constituted through elections. Even today, however, "the state can and often does appear to people in India as a sovereign entity set apart from society.... A local administrative office, a government school, a police station: to enter any of these is to cross the internal boundary into the domain of the state" (Fuller and Harriss 2000: 23).[3] Because national government organizations often appear distant and forbidding, some "expeditor is usually involved who may not be a man with any official power, but he is always someone who is familiar with the intricacies of administration" (Weiner 1963: 123). The mostly ad hoc, opportunistic, and unreliable ways that are currently available for

---

[3] Contacting public officials may be less problematic in Latin American settings. In the pooled eight-nation sample studied by Booth and Seligson, one in six citizens reported contacting legislators or local government officials. The ranges by type of official contacted and between countries, however, varied substantially. Contacting any type of official was reported by as few as 13 percent of Hondurans and as many as 18 percent of Mexicans. Contacting legislative deputies ranged particularly widely, from 8 percent in Mexico to 20 percent in Panama. Such differences quite likely occur because of the differential responsiveness of legislators between countries. Moreover, the social and political distance between a citizen and a legislative deputy in Panama, with only four million people, is much less than that between a citizen and a member of Mexico's Congress in a nation of 105 million. Institutional traits are likely to matter greatly in determining the access of the poor to officials. For example, local officials are much more accessible than national ones. An average of 22 percent of Latin Americans reported having contacted a local official, but the range by country is from a low of only 10 percent of Panamanians to 31 percent of Salvadorans. (Note: This calculation and others in this chapter referencing these eight nations were made by co-author Booth expressly for this chapter.)

making contact and seeking democratic redress hardly bode well for entrenching democracy as the accepted way of organizing public life.

Just as a human body contacts the air through its outermost layer of tissue, the body of democracy interacts with its constituents through its outer ring of institutions and offices. This, we believe, is where democracy becomes real – or not – for the majority of its inhabitants. It is here that everyday insults, injustices, and inequities simmer and could come to a boil when cries for dispossessing the rich are raised.

Providing these voices with democratic succor – making the everyday experience of democracy more democratic in reality – is what we feel it will take for people to lock in their investments in democracy. Social democratic parties went a long way in helping poor people experience democracy in their lives. The accumulated hardship of repeated rulers' rebuffs was whittled away democratically, making democracy stronger in turn. Contextually appropriate institutional solutions, at lower and middle levels of the organizational chart of democracy, are urgently required. Unfortunately, institutional questions are not frequently investigated at these levels. Academics and practitioners of democratic reforms can both contribute a great deal toward enhancing current understandings in this area. Research as well as practice can help us understand better how democracy can be made more democratic – and therefore more respected, legitimate, and abiding – within different cultures and contexts in the developing world.

More is Better

Political institutionalization remains, as Huntington (1968) reminded us, a critically important task, useful as much for moderating and formalizing the demands made by poorer people as for helping make these voices heard in the first place. In poorer countries, converting subjects into citizens requires building – and making widely known and easily accessible – institutional links in the middle, which can facilitate information and promote accountability between citizens and public officials.[4]

---

[4] Examples of institutional innovations that can increase citizen engagement in policy making at the local level are provided by Fung and Wright (2003). Although the

Political parties could play a very important role in this regard, but across the developing world parties are mostly weak and poorly institutionalized. In contemporary Latin America, party systems are breaking down, and parties of the left and labor unions are losing their capacity to represent the interests of poor people because of the constraints imposed on governments by neoliberalism (Jones 2007; Mainwaring and Scully 1995; Weyland 2005). In large parts of South Asia, parties do not have any viable lower- or middle-level organization, at least not of any permanent sort (Kohli 1990; Krishna 2002). Thus, the party-building route to strengthening democracy – especially in the middle and at levels lower down – is not so far progressing in any reassuring manner.

Other forms of middle-level institutions, such as civil society organizations (CSOs) and elected local governments, have been suggested as alternative remedies for filling the institutional gaps in the middle, helping simultaneously both to represent ordinary citizen's demands and to channel these demands in responsible and democratic ways (Booth and Richard 1998; 2006; Edwards, Foley and Diani 2001; Etzioni 2001; Putnam 1993, 2000). Such organizational forms need to be much better explored in developing countries' democracies.

Sadly, these possibilities are sometimes rejected or deemed to be excessively weak. Applying Western understandings of CSOs to measure civil society strength in developing countries has sometimes led to such a conclusion. For example, the World Values Survey of 1991 calculated that although 85 percent of citizens in Sweden, 84 percent in Netherlands, 71 percent in the United States, and 67 percent in West

---

regime of Hugo Chavez in Venezuela is highly controversial for its dismantling of restraints on the executive, it is also aggressively promoting local-level participation by citizens. Canache (2007: 16) explains:

As delineated in Art.70 of the Constitution, direct participation means that the people have the right to use and activate a series of participatory mechanisms, including elections, referenda, citizen legislative initiatives, citizen assemblies, and so on, which are conceived as means of direct citizen participation in political affairs. Beyond this, in the economic and social spheres, this perspective recognizes a protagonist role to the people organized in social organizations such as community organizations, cooperatives, associations, and so on, to participate actively in the decisions concerning their particular needs and affairs.

Germany were members in at least one civic association, the equivalent percentages were much lower in countries of the developing world: 36 percent in Mexico, 24 percent in Argentina, 13 percent in India, and even smaller elsewhere. In the vast rural areas of developing countries, single-digit participation figures were mostly recorded by these kinds of surveys.

There is, however, sharply conflicting evidence on this point. In the surveys of eight Latin American nations reported by Booth and Seligson (in this volume), respondents were asked whether they belonged to any one of four specified types of groups: a church-related, school-related, business, or communal association. Twenty-nine percent of the pooled sample belonged to none of the four types; the remaining, 71 percent, were engaged in at least one of the four types of groups, much higher than the World Values Survey's calculated figure for Latin America. In direct point of comparison to the Mexican results reported for the World Values Survey, 73 percent of Mexicans reported membership in at least one civil society organization – nearly double the percentage found in the other study. The difference is that this survey considered not only formal organizations (following the types that are commonly found in the West) but local-level and informal organizations as well.

Informal organizations – often customary and mostly unregistered – form a very important part of civic association in these countries, and including them showed that civil society was, in fact, much more vibrant. "In much of the developing world, especially in the countryside and rural areas," observes Varshney (2001: 368), "formal associations do not exist. This does not mean, however, that civic interconnections or activities are absent . . . villages make do with informal sites and meetings." For African contexts, Lyon (2000: 677) observed that "formal associations may only be a small factor" in the overall web of organized social interaction. And mapping such informal social organizations in villages of Rajasthan, India, Krishna (2002:5) found that although no more than 7 percent of villagers belonged to any formally registered association, "more than 80 percent of rural residents . . . participate regularly in [informal] labor-sharing groups; 63 percent stated that they had got together with others in the village one or more times in the past year to do something about a community problem." In the eight Latin American nations studied by Booth and Seligson, residents of rural areas are modestly but significantly more active in both civil society (formal) and communal (informal) activism.

It is not clear that such organizations, especially the informal ones, can assume the roles required to be played by the mediating institutions of democracy. But these possibilities need to be explored more fully; indeed, some analyses are upbeat in this regard (e.g., AnanthPur 2004; Shivakumar 2003). As important, civil society organizations and others – including local governments – need to be connected better with the formal mechanisms of democracy. Local governments quite often have weak accountability links working in an upward direction. People can rarely hold councilors accountable, and councilors, in turn, have little voice and less influence at higher levels of government organization. As a result, poor people have little opportunity to air their grievances; they have no place to go where "democracy" hears them and can offer relief (Bayart 1996; Bennett 1986; Hagopian and Mainwaring 2005; Mamdani 1996).

Particularly for poorer people, better functioning middle-level institutions – representative local governments, CSOs, political parties, and the like – offer the best ways in which they can link organically with the formal (and too often, distant) processes of democracy and public decision making. Such middle-level institutions are currently weak, their accountability mechanisms are very weak, and developing more knowledge and better working models of middle-level institutions appropriate to particular contexts and maybe even specific countries is a particularly important remaining task for strengthening democracy in poor countries.

To remain alive, democracy must connect with its parts. Research can help in this effort. Studying how different types of middle-level institutions function in comparative context can help provide better guidance for such institution building efforts that are sorely required. Most usually, research in developing countries has examined single institutional types, focusing on the separate merits of decentralized local governments, indigenous organizations, or NGOs. Although more such research needs to be done, one also needs to examine more directly how these institutions work in tandem, how the entire patchwork of subordinate institutions works (or not) in particular situations. Providing more systematic information about which middle-level institutions work better (when and where) is an important service that researchers can help provide.

There are still too many instances of paper democracies, with a modicum of democratic rights being expressed every four to five years and neglect or repression remaining over the long periods in between. Making democracy work better for poorer people requires providing them with better institutional tools.

Choices among alternative institutional forms should not be ideologically but pragmatically driven. The idea of providing diverse, integrative participation opportunities for ordinary citizens is an old one, both in theory and in fact. Swiss communards of the Middle Ages took part in every aspect of the lives of their communities and largely successfully defended their commonly owned and managed economic resources and governments from the encroachment of feudalism. John Stuart Mill (1958) advocated that democracies provide multiple institutional opportunities for ordinary, uneducated citizens to discharge public functions. Interesting experiments in giving civil society and poorer citizens formal roles in local and regional policy making have been attempted in Cuba and Nicaragua during their revolutions, in Peru during the period of left-populist military rule during the late 1960s and early 1970s, and are under way in Venezuela today.[5] Yugoslavia undertook one of the most extensive experiments with citizen participation in the workplace and at the local level during the 1960s (Pateman 1970). These exercises have not been linked, however, to liberal democratic forms, and have tended to vanish upon the demise of the leftist governments that sponsored them.

Diverse institutional forms will likely be more useful as they follow and advance two key principles (or longer-term goals). *Equality of access* in the political realm is a worthy goal that diverse middle-level institutions can help promote. Citizens more assured of having

[5] See, for instance, various chapters on Peru in Seligson and Booth (1979). See also Booth (1985) and Canache (1998).

influence through acting within democratic channels are less likely to turn to undemocratic means. In the economic realm, the parallel goal is improved *equality of opportunity*. Existing inequality may not seem so intolerable when poorer citizens see reason to believe that for their children at least, if not also for themselves, the future is filled with brighter prospects. "Because talent and ideas are widely distributed in the population, a prosperous modern society requires the mass of people to have incentives – and a state that can and will provide key complementary inputs and public goods" (World Bank, 2006: 124).

Identifying the conditions leading to breakdown of democracy, Przeworski (in this volume) advances the view that "if no redistribution simultaneously satisfies the poor and the wealthy and if either group has any chance to establish its dictatorship, democracy cannot be sustained." Working to remedy gross inequalities – while remaining vigilant to the danger that some groups might find dictatorship attractive – is important for helping root democracy more firmly in the world.

Rectifying inequality through redistribution of assets may not be an achievable goal in many contexts, and it may involve the additional risk of sacrificing democracy, but redistributing opportunity more fairly and equitably is a more feasible policy objective. It is more likely that inequality will be borne stoically by poorer people, and the dangers of elite reaction will become commensurately reduced, when opportunity is widely available and social mobility is seen as a real possibility for all. The middle class grows through promoting equality of opportunity, and having larger middle classes has been shown to work positively for democracy (Bueno de Mesquita and Downs 2005; Lipset 1981).

Education is doubly important, thus, for democratic strengthening. Directly, it raises public support for democracy, and indirectly, through promoting equality of opportunity, education helps grow the middle class in a society.

Focusing on processes and not just outcomes is important for achieving the longer-term goals of equal opportunity and equal access. Helpful middle-level institutions are required for achieving both these goals. Accountability will remain merely a buzzword until its institutional underpinnings are put in place, and equal opportunity will not be realized until institutions facilitate and enforce it with regularity.

New institutions need to be pioneered that can serve the representation and demand-making needs of poor people. The Nobel Prize-winning example of the Grameen Bank shows that institutional innovation is both necessary and possible. The institutions of banking developed in the West do not work as well – and often do not work at all – for poor people in poorer countries. A new banking institution needed to be developed, complete with new products and new procedures, new roles and new normative understandings. Providing access to institutionalized credit helped displace usurious moneylenders. Providing institutionalized access to democracy will help replace the "big men."

Institutions to retail democracy to the poor in developing countries need to be pioneered and put in place, assisted by careful scholarship. Research and practice can help uncover new and helpful institutional forms, modifying and advancing the learning acquired in these respects in the West. Investments in education need to be pushed harder, considering on the credit side not only the economic and social payoffs of these investments but also the benefits that accrue in terms of stronger democracy and more democratic governance.

Bibliography

Abraham, David. 1987. *The Breakdown of the Weimar Republic: Political Economy and Crisis*. Princeton, NJ: Princeton University Press.

Abramson, Paul. R. 1983. *Political Attitudes in America: Formation and Change*. San Francisco: Freeman.

Acemoglu, Daron and James A. Robinson. 2006. *Economic Origins of Dictatorship and Democracy*. New York: Cambridge University Press.

Adams, Richard Newbold. 1979. The Structure of Participation: A Commentary. In *Politics and the Poor: Political Participation in Latin America*, edited by Mitchell A. Seligson and John A. Booth: 9–17. New York: Holmes and Meier.

Adorno, Theodor, Daniel J. Levinson, Else Frenkel-Brunswik, and R. Nevitt Sanford. 1950. *The Authoritarian Personality*. New York: Harper & Row.

Afrobarometer. 2002. Key Findings about Public Opinion in Africa. Afrobarometer Briefing Paper No. 1. http://www.afrobarometer.org

Afrobarometer Network. 2004. Afrobarometer Round 2: Compendium of Comparative Results from a 15-Country Survey. Afrobarometer Working Paper No. 34. http://www.afrobarometer.org

Ake, Claude. 1996. *Democracy and Development in Africa*. Washington, DC: The Brookings Institution.

Alkire, Sabina. 2002. *Valuing Freedoms: Sen's Capability Approach and Poverty Reduction*. Oxford: Oxford University Press.

Almond, Gabriel A. 1954. *The Appeals of Communism*. Princeton, NJ: Princeton University Press.

Almond, Gabriel A. and Sydney Verba. 1963. *The Civic Culture: Political Attitudes and Democracy in Five Nations*. Princeton, NJ: Princeton University Press.

———. 1965. *The Civic Culture: Political Attitudes and Democracy in Five Nations*. Boston: Little, Brown.

Altemeyer, Robert. 1981. *Right-Wing Authoritarianism*. Winnipeg, MB, Canada: University of Manitoba Press.

———. 1996. *The Authoritarian Specter*. Cambridge, MA: Harvard University Press.

———. 2004. Highly Dominating, Highly Authoritarian Personalities. *Journal of Social Psychology* 144 (4): 421–47.

———. 2006. *The Authoritarians*. http://members.shaw.ca/jeanaltemeyer/drbob/TheAuthoritarians.pdf

AnanthPur, Kripa. 2004. Rivalry or Synergy? Formal and Informal Local Governance in Rural India. IDS Working Paper 226. Institute of Development Studies, Brighton, UK.

Anduiza Perea, Eva. 1999. *Individuos o sistemas? Las razones de la abstención en Europa Occidental*. Madrid: Centro de Investigaciones Sociológicas.

Apter, David E. 1965. *The Politics of Modernization*. Chicago and London: University of Chicago Press.

Arat, Zehra F. 1988. Democracy and Economic Development: Modernization Theory Revisited. *Comparative Politics* 21: 21–36.

Atkinson, Anthony B. 1987. On the Measurement of Poverty. *Econometrica* 55 (4): 749–64.

Bachrach, Peter. 1966. The Theory of Democratic Elitism. Boston: Little, Brown.

Bagehot, Walter. 1963. *The English Constitution*. Ithaca, NY: Cornell University Press.

Barro, Robert. 1996. Democracy and Growth. *Journal of Economic Growth* 1: 1–27.

———. 1997. *Determinants of Economic Growth*. Cambridge, MA: MIT Press.

Bayart, Jean-Francois. 1996. *The State in Africa: The Politics of the Belly*. New York: Longman.

Benhabib, Jess and Adam Przeworski. 2006. The political economy of redistribution under democracy. Special Issue, *Economic Theory*.

Bennett, Stephen E. 1986. *Apathy in America 1960–1984: Causes and Consequences of Citizen Political Indifference*. New York: Transnational.

Bernhard, Michael, Timothy Nordstrom, and Christopher Reenock. 2001. Economic Performance, Institutional Intermediation, and Democratic Survival. *Journal of Politics* 63 (3): 775–803.

Bhalla, Surjit S. 1994, August. Freedom and Economic Growth: A Virtuous Circle? Paper presented at the Nobel Symposium, Democracy's Victory and Crisis, Uppsala University, Sweden.

Biles, Robert A. 1978. Political Participation in Urban Uruguay: Mixing Public and Private Ends. In *Citizen and State: Political Participation in Latin America*, edited by John A. Booth and Mitchell A. Seligson: 85–97. New York: Holmes and Meier.

Bilson, John F. 1982. Civil Liberty – An Econometric Investigation. *Kyklos* 35 (1): 94–114.

Bimber, Bruce A. 2003. *Information and American Democracy: Technology in the Evolution of Political Power*. New York: Cambridge University Press.

Bobo, Lawrence and Gilliam, Franklin D. 1990. Race, Sociopolitical Participation, and Black Empowerment. *American Political Science Review* 84: 377–93.

Boix, Carles. 2003. *Democracy and Redistribution*. Cambridge: Cambridge University Press.

Boix, Carles and Susan Stokes. 2003. Endogenous Democratization. *World Politics* 55 (4): 517–49.

Bollen, Kenneth and Robert Jackman. 1985. Political Democracy and the Size Distribution of Income. *American Sociological Review* 50: 438–57.

Booth, John A. 1976. A Replication: Modes of Political Participation in Costa Rica. *Western Political Quarterly* 29 (December): 627–33.

———. 1978. Are Latin Americans Politically Rational? Citizen Participation and Democracy in Costa Rica. In *Citizen and State: Political Participation in Latin America*, edited by John A. Booth and Mitchell A. Seligson: 98–113. New York: Holmes and Meier.

———. 1979. Political Participation in Latin America: Levels, Structure, Context, Concentration, and Rationality. *Latin American Research Review* 14, (Fall): 29–60.

———.1985. *The End and the Beginning: The Nicaraguan Revolution*. Boulder, CO: Westview Press.

———. 1998. *Costa Rica: Quest for Democracy*. Boulder, CO: Westview Press.

———. 2006, March 17. Sociopolitical Violence, Protest, and Antidemocratic and Confrontational Norms in Eight Latin American Nations. Paper presented at the Latin American Studies Association, San Juan, Puerto Rico.

———. 2007, April 6. Social and Political Capital in Latin American Democracies. Paper presented at the Symposium on the Prospects for Democracy in Latin America. Denton, TX.

Booth, John A. and Patricia Bayer Richard. 1998. Civil Society, Political Capital, and Democratization in Central America. *Journal of Politics* 60 (3): 780–800.

———. 2006. Violence, Participation, and Democratic Norms: Prospects for Democratic Consolidation in Post-Conflict Central America. In *Conflict Prevention and Peacebuilding in Post-War Societies*, edited by T. David Mason and James D. Meernik: 196–218. London: Routledge.

Booth, John A. and Mitchell A. Seligson. 1978a. Images of Participation in Latin America. In *Citizen and State: Political Participation in Latin America*, Vol. 1., edited by John A. Booth and Mitchell A. Seligson, 3–33. New York: Holmes and Meir.

Booth, John A. and Mitchell A. Seligson, eds. 1978b. *Citizen and State: Political Participation in Latin America*, vol.1. New York: Holmes and Meier.

Booth, John A. and Mitchell A. Seligson. 1979. Peasants as Activists: A Reevaluation of Political Participation in the Countryside. *Comparative Political Studies* 12: 29–59.

———. 1984. The Political Culture of Authoritarianism in Mexico: A Reevaluation. *Latin American Research Review* 19 (1): 106–24.

———. 2005. Political Legitimacy and Participation in Costa Rica: Evidence of Arena Shopping. *Political Research Quarterly* 59 (4): 537–50.

Booth, John A., Christine J. Wade, and Thomas W. Walker. (2006). *Understanding Central America: Global Forces, Rebellion and Change*. Boulder, CO: Westview Press.

Booth, John A., Mitchell A. Seligson, and Miguel Goméz Barrantes. 2006. Os Contornos Da Cidadanía Crítica: Explorando a Legitimidade Democrática: *Opinião Pública* 12 (1).

———. 2005. The Structure of Democratic Legitimacy. Manuscript (April).

Bourque, Susan C. and Kay B. Warren. 1979. Female Participation, Perception, and Power: An Examination of Two Andean Communities. In *Political Participation in Latin America: Politics and the Poor*, edited by Mitchell A. Seligson and John A. Booth: 116–133. New York: Holmes and Meier

Bratton, Michael. 2004. The Alternation Effect in Africa. *Journal of Democracy* 15 (4): 147–158.

Bratton, Michael, Yun-han Chu, and Marta Lagos. 2006. Who Votes? Implications for New Democracies. www.globalbarometer.net

Bratton, Michael and Robert Mattes. 2001a. Africans' Surprising Universalism. *Journal of Democracy* 12: 107–21.

———. 2001b. Support for Democracy in Africa: Intrinsic or Instrumental? *British Journal of Political Science* 31: 447–74.

Bratton, Michael, Robert Mattes, and E. Gyimah-Boadi. 2005. *Public Opinion, Democracy, and Market Reform in Africa*. New York: Cambridge University Press.

Bratton, Michael and Nicolas vande Walle. 1997. *Democratic Experiments in Africa: Regime Transitions in Comparative Perspective*. New York: Cambridge University Press.

Brown, David S. and Wendy Hunter. 2004. Democracy and Human Capital Formation: Education Spending in Latin America, 1980–1997. *Comparative Political Studies* 37 (7): 842–64.

Bueno de Mesquita, Bruce and George W. Downs. 2005. Development and Democracy. *Foreign Affairs*, September/October: 77–86.

Bunce, Valerie J. 2000. Comparative Democratization: Big and Bounded Generalizations. *Comparative Political Studies* 33: 703–34.

Campbell, Angus, Philip E. Converse, Warren E. Miller, and Donald E. Stokes. 1960. *The American Voter*. New York: Wiley.

Canache, Damarys. (2007, April). *Chavismo* and Democracy in Venezuela. Paper presented at the Symposium on the Prospects for Democracy in Latin America. Denton, TX.

——. 1998, *Reinventing Legitimacy: Democracy and Political Change in Venezuela*. Westport, Conn.: Greenwood Press.

Carstairs, R. 1912. *The Little World of an Indian District Officer*. London: Macmillan.

Chabal, Patrick and Jean-Pascal Daloz. 1999. *Africa Works: Disorder as Political Instrument*. Bloomington: Indiana University Press.

Chambers, Robert. 1983. *Rural Development: Putting the Last First*. London: Longman.

——. 1988. Poverty in India: Concepts, Research and Reality. Discussion Paper 241. Brighton, UK: Institute of Development Studies.

Chatterjee, Partha. 2004. *The Politics of the Governed: Reflections on Popular Politics in Most of the World*. New York: Columbia University Press.

Clark, David. 2002. *Visions of Development: A Study of Human Values*. Cheltenham, UK: Edward Elgar.

Clark, David and David Hulme. 2005. Towards a Unified Framework for Understanding the Depth, Breadth and Duration of Poverty. Working Paper No. 20, Global Research Group, Institute for Development Policy and Management, University of Manchester, UK.

Cohen, Carl. 1973. *Democracy*. New York: The Free Press.

Collier, Ruth Berins. 1999. *Paths Toward Democracy: The Working Class and Elites in Western Europe and South America*. New York: Cambridge University Press.

Collini, Stefan, Donald Winch, and John Burrow. 1983. *That Noble Science of Politics*. Cambridge: Cambridge University Press.

Condorcet, Antoine Nicolas. 1785/1986. Essai sur l'application de l'analyse a la probabilité des décisions rendues a la pluralité des voix. In *Sur les élections et autres textes*, textes choisis et revus par Olivier de Bernon, 9–176. Paris: Fayard.

Conway, Margaret. 2000. *Political Participation in the United States*. Washington, DC: Congressional Quarterly.

Coppedge, Michael. 1997. Modernization and Thresholds of Democracy: Evidence for a Common Path and Process. In *Inequality, Democracy, and Economic Development*, edited by Manus I. Midlarsky: 177–201. Cambridge: Cambridge University Press.

Cornelius, Wayne A. 1974. Urbanization and Political Demand-Making: Political Participation among the Migrant Poor in Latin American Cities. *American Political Science Review* 68 (September): 1125–46.

Coser, Lewis. 1956. *The Functions of Social Conflict*. Glencoe, IL: Free Press.

Crook, Malcolm. 1996. *Elections in the French Revolution*. Cambridge: Cambridge University Press.

Cutwright, Phillips. 1963. National Political Development: Measurement and Analysis. *American Sociological Review* 28: 42–59.

Dahl, Robert A. 1971. *Polyarchy: Participation and Opposition.* New Haven, CT: Yale University Press.

———. (1989). *Democracy and Its Critics.* New Haven, CT: Yale University Press.

Dalton, Russell J. 1999. Political Support in Advanced Industrial Democracies. In *Critical Citizens: Global Support for Democratic Government*, edited by Pippa Norris, 57–77. New York: Oxford University Press.

———. 2004. *Democratic Challenges, Democratic Choices: The Erosion of Political Support in Advanced Industrial Democracies.* Oxford: Oxford University Press.

Dasgupta, Partha. 1996. *An Inquiry into Well-Being and Destitution.* Oxford: Oxford University Press.

Davis, Richard. 1998. *The Web of Politics.* Oxford: Oxford University Press.

Deininger, Klaus and Lyn Squire. 1996. A New Data Set Measuring Income Inequality. *World Bank Economic Review*: 565–91.

Dekker, Paul and Peter Ester. 1987. Working-Class Authoritarianism: A Reexamination of the Lipset Thesis. *European Journal of Political Research*, 15 (2): 395–415.

———. 1990. Authoritarianism and the Concept of Class: A Reply to Middendorp and Meloen. *European Journal of Political Research* 18 (2): 269–275.

Delli Carpini, Michael X. and Scott Keeter. 1996. *What Americans Know about Politics and Why It Matters.* New Haven, CT: Yale University Press.

Diamond, Larry. 1992. Economic Development and Democracy Reconsidered. In *Reexamining Democracy: Essays in Honor of Seymour Martin Lipset*, edited by Gary Marks and Larry Diamond, 93–139. London: Sage.

———. 1999. *Developing Democracy: Toward Consolidation.* Baltimore: Johns Hopkins University Press.

Diamond, Larry, Juan Linz, and Seymour M. Lipset. 1995. Introduction: What Makes for Democracy. In *Politics in Developing Countries: Comparing Experiences with Democracy*, edited by Larry Diamond, Juan Linz, and Seymour Lipset, 1–66. Boulder, CO: Lynne Rienner.

Dunn, Susan. 2004. *Jefferson's Second Revolution: The Election Crisis of 1800 and the Triumph of Republicanism.* Boston: Houghton Mifflin.

Easterly, William and Ross Levine. 1997. Africa's Growth Tragedy: Policies and Ethnic Divisions. *Quarterly Journal of Economics* 113: 1203–50.

Easton, David. 1965. *A Framework of Political Analysis.* Englewood Cliffs, NJ: Prentice-Hall.

———. 1968. *The Political System.* New York: Alfred A. Knopf.

———. 1975. A Re-Assessment of the Concept of Political Support. *British Journal of Political Science* 5: 435–57.

Edwards, Bob, Michael W. Foley, and Mario Diani, eds. 2001. Beyond Toc-queville: Civil Society and the Social Capital Debate in *Comparative Perspective*. Medford, MA: Tufts University Press of New England.

Etzioni, Amitai. 2001. *Next: The Road to the Good Society*. New York: Basic Books.

Evans, Geoffrey and Pauline Rose. (2007). Support for Democracy in Malawi: Does Schooling Matter? *World Development* 35 (5): 904–19

Ferejohn, John A. and James H. Kuklinski. 1990. *Information and Democratic Processes*. Chicago: University of Chicago Press.

Figueiredo, Argelina. 1993. *Democracia ou reformas: Alternativas demo-cráticas à crise política*. São Paulo, Brazil: Paz e Terra.

Finkel, Steven E. 1985. Reciprocal Effects of Participation and Political Efficacy. *American Journal of Political Science* 29: 891–913.

———. 1987. The Effects of Participation on Political Efficacy and Political Support: Evidence from a West German Panel. *Journal of Politics* 49: 441–64.

———. 2002. Civic Education and the Mobilization of Political Participation in Developing Democracies. *Journal of Politics* 64: 994–1020.

Fishel, John T. 1979. Political Participation in a Peruvian Highland District. In *Political Participation in Latin America: Politics and the Poor*, edited by Mitchell A. Seligson and John A. Booth: 51–61. New York: Holmes and Meier.

Fox, Jonathan, ed. 1990. *The Challenge of Rural Democratization: Perspectives from Latin America and the Philippines*. London: Frank Cass.

Franklin, Mark N. 2004. *Voter Turnout and the Dynamics of Electoral Competition in Established Democracies since 1945*. Cambridge: Cambridge University Press.

Freedom House. 2005a. Freedom in the World 2003: Country and Related Territory Reports 2004. http://freedomhouse.org/research/freeworld/2003/countries.htm

Freedom House. 2005b. Country Reports. http://freedomhouse.org/template.cfm?page=21&year=2005

Friedman, Stephen. 2002. Democracy, Inequality and the Reconstitution of Politics. In *Democratic Governance and Social Inequality*, edited by Joseph S. Tulchin, 13–40. Boulder, CO: Lynne Rienner.

Fuller, Christopher J. and John Harriss. (2000). "For an Anthropology of the Modern Indian State," pp. 1–30 in Fuller, C.J. and V. Benei, eds., *The Everyday State and Society in Modern India*. New Delhi: Social Science Press.

Fung, Archon and Eric Olin Wright. 2001. Deepening Democracy: Innovations in Empowered Participatory Governance. *Politics & Society*, 29 (1): 5–41.

———. 2003. *Deepening Democracy: Institutional Innovations in Empowered Participatory Governance*. London: Verso.

Gargarella, Roberto. 2005. *Los fundamentos legales de la desigualdad: El constitucionalismo en América (1776–1860)*. Madrid: Siglo XXI.

Garrido, Aurora. 1998. Electors and Electoral Districts in Spain, 1874–1936. In *How Did They Become Voters? The History of Franchise in Modern European Representation*, edited by Raffaele Romanelli, 207–226. The Hague: Kluwer.

Gasiorowski, Mark J. 1995. Economic Crisis and Political Regime Change: An Event History Analysis. *American Political Science Review* 89 (4): 882–97.

Gaviria, Alejandro, Ugo Panizza, and Jessica Seddon. 2002. Economic, Social and Demographic Determinants on Political Participation in Latin America: Evidence from the 1990s. Working Paper 472, Inter-American Development Bank, Washington, DC.

Geddes, Barbara. 1994. *Politician's Dilemma: Building State Capacity in Latin America*. Berkeley: University of California Press.

Gibson, James and Amanda Gouws. 2003. *Overcoming Intolerance in South Africa: Experiments in Democratic Persuasion*. New York: Cambridge University Press.

Goodrich, Melanie and Jonathan Nagler. 2006. A Good Model of Turnout and a Cross-National Empirical Analysis. Manuscript. Department of Politics, New York University.

Graham, Richard. 2003. Ciudadanía y jerarquía en el Brasil esclavista. In *Ciudadaní política y formación de las naciones: Perspectivas históricas de América Latina*, edited by Hilda Sabato, 345–370. Mexico City: El Colegio de Mexico.

Granato, Jim, Ronald Inglehart, and David Leblang. 1996. Cultural Values, Stable Democracy, and Economic Development: A Reply. *American Journal of Political Science* 40: 680–696.

Grugel, Jean. 2002. *Democratization: A Critical Introduction*. New York: Palgrave.

Gutiérrez Sanin, Francisco. 2003. La literatura plebeya y el debate alrededor de la propriedad (Nueva Granada, 1849–1854). In *Ciudadaní política y formación de las naciones: Perspectivas históricas de América Latina*, edited by Hilda Sabato, 181–201. Mexico City: El Colegio de Mexico.

Hachhethu, Krishna. 2005. What the People Feel. *Seminar*, 548 (April): 62–8.

Hagopian, Frances. 2000. Political Development Revisited. *Comparative Political Studies* 33 (6/7), 880–911.

Hagopian, Frances and Scott Mainwaring, eds. 2005. *The Third Wave of Democratization in Latin America*. New York: Cambridge University Press.

Harrington, Michael. 1962. *The Other America*. New York: Macmillan.

Heath, Anthony, Stephen Fisher, and Shawna Smith. 2005. The Globalization of Public Opinion Research. *Annual Review of Political Science* 8: 297–333.

Helliwell, John F. 1994. Empirical Linkages between Democracy and Economic Growth. *British Journal of Political Science* 24, 225–48.

Herrera, Javier, Mireille Razafindrakoto, and Francois Roubaud. 2006. *Governance, Democracy and Poverty Reduction: Lessons Drawn from Household Surveys in sub-Saharan Africa and Latin America*. Paris: Ministere des Affaires etrangeres.

Hill, David. 2006. *American Voter Turnout: An Institutional Perspective.* Boulder, CO: Westview Press.

Hiskey, Jonathan T. and Shaun Bowler. 2005. Local Context and Democratization in Mexico. *American Journal of Political Science* 49: 57–71.

Hiskey, Jonathan T. and Mitchell A. Seligson. 2003. Pitfalls of Power to the People: Decentralization, Local Government Performance, and System Support in Bolivia. *Studies in Comparative International Development* 37: 64–88.

Hulme David and John Toye. (2006). The Case for Cross-Disciplinary Social Science Research on Poverty, Inequality and Well-Being. *Journal of Development Studies* 42 (7): 1085–1107.

Huntington, Samuel P. 1968. *Political Order in Changing Societies*. New Haven, CT: Yale University Press.

———. 1971. The Change to Change: Modernization, Development, and Politics. *Comparative Politics* 3 (3): 283–322.

———. 1984. Will More Countries Become Democracies? *Political Science Quarterly* 99: 193–218.

———. 1991. *The Third Wave: Democratization in the Late Twentieth Century*. Norman: University of Oklahoma Press.

Huntington, Samuel P. and Joan M. Nelson. 1976. *No Easy Choice: Political Participation in Developing Countries*. Cambridge, MA: Harvard University Press.

Hyden, Goran. 1983. *No Shortcuts to Progress: African Development Management in Perspective*. Berkeley: University of California Press.

Inglehart, Ronald. 1990. *Culture Shift in Advanced Industrial Society*. Princeton, NJ: Princeton University Press.

———. 1997. *Modernization and Postmodernization: Cultural, Economic and Political Change in 43 Societies*. Princeton, NJ: Princeton University Press.

Inglehart, Ronald and Wayne E. Baker. 2000. Modernization, Cultural Change, and the Persistence of Traditional Values. *American Sociological Review* 65: 19–51.

Inglehart, Ronald and Christian Welzel. 2005. *Modernization, Cultural Change, and Democracy: The Human Development Sequence*. New York: Cambridge University Press.

Iyengar, Shanto and Donald R. Kinder. 1987. *News that Matters: Television and American Public Opinion*. Chicago: University of Chicago Press.

Jackman, Robert W. 1987. Political Institutions and Voter Turnout in the Industrial Democracies. *American Political Science Review* 81: 405–23.

Jackman, Robert W. and Ross A. Miller. 1995. Voter Turnout in the Industrial Democracies During the 1980s. *Comparative Political Studies* 27: 467–92.

Jackman, Robert W. and Ross A. Miller. 1996. A Renaissance of Political Culture? *American Journal of Political Science* 40: 632–659.

Jackson, Robert A. 1995. Clarifying the Relationship between Education and Turnout. *American Politics Quarterly* 23: 279–99.

———. 2003. Differential Influences on Latino Electoral Participation. *Political Behavior* 25: 339–66.

Jaffrelot, Christophe. 2003. *India's Silent Revolution: The Rise of the Low Castes in North Indian Politics*. New Delhi: Permanent Black.

Jodha, N. S. 1988. Poverty Debate in India: A Minority View. *Economic and Political Weekly Bombay* November: 2421–28.

Jones, Mark. 2007, April. Political Parties and Party Systems in Latin America. Paper presented at the Symposium on the Prospects for Democracy in Latin America. Denton, TX.

Karatnycky, Adrian. 2004. National Income and Liberty. *Journal of Democracy* 15: 82–93.

Ketcham, Ralph, ed. 1986. *The Anti-Federalist Papers and the Constitutional Convention Debates*. New York: Mentor Books.

Kim, Wonik. 2004. The Political Economy of Unemployment Insurance. PhD diss., Department of Politics, New York University.

Kohli, Atul. 1987. *The State and Poverty in India: The Politics of Reform*. Cambridge: Cambridge University Press.

———. 1990. *Democracy and Discontent: India's Growing Crisis of Governability*. Cambridge: Cambridge University Press.

Krishna, Anirudh. 2002. *Active Social Capital: Tracing the Roots of Development and Democracy*. New York: Columbia University Press.

———. 2003. What is Happening to Caste? A View from Some North Indian Villages. *Journal of Asian Studies* 62 (4): 1171–93.

———. 2004. Escaping Poverty and Becoming Poor: Who Gains, Who Loses, and Why? *World Development* 32 (1): 121–36.

———. 2006a. Reversal of Fortune: Why Preventing Poverty Beats Curing It. *Foreign Policy* (May/June): 62–65.

———. 2006b. Poverty and Democratic Participation Reconsidered: Evidence from the Local Level in India. *Comparative Politics* 38 (4), 439–58.

Krishna, Anirudh, Daniel Lumonya, Milissa Markiewicz, Firminus Mugumya, Agatha Kafuko, and Jonah Wegoye. 2006, Escaping Poverty and Becoming Poor in 36 Villages of Central and Western Uganda. *Journal of Development Studies* 42 (2): 346–70.

Krishna, Anirudh, Norman Thomas Uphoff, and Milton J. Esman. 1997. *Reasons for Hope: Instructive Experiences in Rural Development*. West Hartford, CT: Kumarian Press.

Lal, Deepak, Rakesh Mohan, and I. Natarajan, 2001. Economic Reform and Poverty Alleviation: A Tale of Two Surveys. *Economic and Political Weekly* (March 24): 1017–28.

Landa, Dimitri and Ethan B. Kapstein. 2001. Inequality, Growth and Democracy. *World Politics* 53: 264–96.

Landsberger, Henry A., and Bobby M. Gierisch. 1979. Political and Economic Activism: Peasant Participation in the *Ejidos* of the Comarca Lagunera of Mexico. In *Political Participation in Latin America: Politics and the Poor*, edited by Mitchell A. Seligson and John A. Booth. 76–96. New York: Holmes and Meier.

Laswell, Harold D. 1946. *Power and Personality*. New York.

Lehoucq, Fabrice Edouard and Iván Molina Jiménez. 2002. *Stuffing the Ballot Box: Fraud, Electoral Reform, and Democratization in Costa Rica. Cambridge Studies in Comparative Politics*. New York: Cambridge University Press.

LeoGrande, William. 1978. Mass Political Participation in Social Cuba. In *Political Participation in Latin America: Citizen and State*, edited by Mitchell Seligson and John A. Booth, 114–128. New York: Holmes and Meier.

Lerner, Daniel. 1958. *The Passing of Traditional Society: Modernizing the Middle East*. New York: Free Press.

Lewis, Oscar. (1963). *The Children of Sanchez*. New York: Random House.

Lewis-Beck, Michael, and Ross E. Burkhart. 1994. Comparative Democracy: The Economic Development Thesis. *American Political Science Review* 88: 903–10.

Lijphart, Arend. 1997. Unequal Participation: Democracy's Unresolved Dilemma. *American Political Science Review* 91: 1–14.

Linz, Juan J. and Alfred Stepan. 1978. *The Breakdown of Democratic Regimes: Europe*. Baltimore: The Johns Hopkins University Press.

———. 1996. *Problems of Democratic Transition and Consolidation: Southern Europe, South America, and Post-Communist Europe*. Baltimore: Johns Hopkins University Press.

Lipset, Seymour M. 1959a. Some Social Requisites of Democracy: Economic Development and Political Legitimacy. *American Political Science Review* 53: 69–105.

———. 1959b. Democracy and Working-Class Authoritarianism. *American Sociological Review* 24: 482–502.

———. 1960. *Political Man: The Social Bases of Politics*. Garden City, NY: Doubleday.

———. 1963. *Political Man: The Social Bases of Politics*. New York: Anchor Books (reprint).

———. 1981. *Political Man: The Social Bases of Politics*. (Expanded edition). Baltimore: Johns Hopkins University Press.

————. 1994. The Social Requisites of Democracy Revisited. *American Sociological Review* 59, 1–22.

Lipset, Seymour M., Kyoung-Ryung Seong, and John Charles Torres. 1993. A Comparative Analysis of the Social Requisites of Democracy. *International Social Science Journal* 136: 155–75.

Logan, Carolyn and Michael Bratton. 2006. The Political Gender Gap in Africa: Similar Attitudes, Different Behaviors. Afrobarometer Working Paper No. 58. www.afrobarometer.org

Londregan, John B. and Keith T. Poole. 1996. Does High Income Promote Democracy? *World Politics* 49: 56–91.

Lyon, Fergus. 2000. "Trust, Networks and Norms: The Creation of Social Capital in Agricultural Economies in Ghana." *World Development*, 28 (4), 663–681.

Macaulay, Thomas B. 1900. *Complete Writings*, vol. 17. Boston and New York: Houghton Mifflin.

Mainwaring, Scott and A. Perez-Linan. 2003. Level of Development and Democracy: Latin American Exceptionalism, 1945–1996. *Comparative Political Studies* 36 (9): 1031–67.

Mainwaring, Scott and Timothy R. Scully, eds. 1995. *Building Democratic Institutions: Party Systems in Latin America*. Stanford, CA: Stanford University Press.

Mamdani, Mahmood. 1996. *Citizen and Subject: Contemporary Africa and the Legacy of Late Colonialism*. Princeton, NJ: Princeton University Press.

Manin, Bernard. 1997. *The Principles of Representative Government*. Cambridge: Cambridge University Press.

Manor, James G. 2000. Small-Time Political Fixers in India's States. *Asian Survey* 40 (5): 816–35.

Martin, John Levi. 2001. The Authoritarian Personality, 50 Years Later: What Questions Are There for Political Psychology? *Political Psychology* 22 (1): 1–26.

Marx, Karl. 1850/1952. *Class Struggles in France, 1848 to 1850*. Moscow: Progress Publishers.

Marx, Karl. 1851/1934. *The Eighteenth Brumaire of Louis Bonaparte*. Moscow: Progress Publishers.

Mattes, Robert, Michael Bratton, and Yul D. Davids. 2003. Poverty, Survival, and Democracy in Southern Africa. Afrobarometer Working Paper No. 23. http://www.afrobarometer.org

Mayer, A. 1997. Caste in an Indian Village: Change and Continuity 1954–1992. In *Caste Today*, edited by C. J. Fuller., 32–64. New Delhi: Oxford University Press.

Maza Valenzuela, Erika. 1995. Catolicismo, Anticlericalismo y la Extensión del Sufragio a la Mujer en Chile. *Estudios Politicos* 58: 137–97.

Middendorp, Cees and J. D. Meloen. 1990. The Authoritarianism of the Working Class Revisited. *European Journal of Political Research* 18 (2): 257–67.

Milbrath, Lester. 1965. *Political Participation: How and Why Do People Get Involved in Politics?* Chicago: Rand McNally.

Miliband, Ralph. 1975. *Parliamentary Socialism.* London: New Left Books.

Mill, John Stuart. 1958. *Considerations on Representative Government.* Indianapolis, IN: Bobbs-Merrill.

―――. 1991. *Considerations on Representative Government.* Buffalo, NY: Prometheus Books.

Mitra, Subrata. 1991. Room to Maneuver in the Middle: Local Elites, Political Action, and the State in India. *World Politics* 43 (April): 390–413.

Montesquieu, Charles. 1748/1995. *De l'Esprit des Lois* [The Spirit of Laws]. Paris: Gallimard.

Moore, Richard J. 1979. The Urban Poor in Guayaquil, Ecuador: Modes, Correlates, and Context of Political Participation. In *Political Participation in Latin America: Politics and the Poor,* edited by Mitchell A. Seligson and John A. Booth. 198–218. New York: Holmes and Meier.

Mueller, J. 1992. Democracy and Ralph's Pretty Good Grocery: Elections, Equality, and the Minimal Human Being. *American Journal of Political Science* 36: 983–1003.

Muller, Edward N. 1988. Democracy, Economic Development, and Income Inequality. *American Sociological Review* 53: 50–68.

―――. 1997. Economic Determinants of Democracy. In *Inequality, Democracy, and Economic Development,* edited by Manus I. Midlarsky. 133–155. Cambridge: Cambridge University Press.

Muller, Edward N. and Mitchell A. Seligson. 1994. Civil Culture and Democracy: The Question of Causal Relationships. *American Political Science Review* 88: 635–52.

Narayan, Deepa, Robert Chambers, Meera Kaul Shah, and Patti Petesch. 2000. *Voices of the Poor: Crying Out for Change.* New York: Oxford University Press for the World Bank.

Newton, Kenneth. 1999. Social and Political Trust in Established Democracies. In *Critical Citizens: Global Support for Democratic Governance,* edited by Pippa Norris, 169–87. New York: Oxford University Press.

Nie, Norman, Jane Junn and Kenneth Stehlik-Barry. 1996. *Education and Democratic Citizenship in America.* Chicago: University of Chicago Press.

Norris, Pippa. 1999a. Conclusions: The Growth of Critical Citizens and its Consequences. In *Critical Citizens: Global Support for Democratic Governance,* edited by Pippa Norris, 257–72. New York: Oxford University Press.

Norris, Pippa. ed. 1999b. *Critical Citizens: Global Support for Democratic Government.* Oxford: Oxford University Press.

Norris, Pippa. 2000. *A Virtuous Circle: Political Communications in Post-Industrial Societies.* New York: Cambridge University Press.

―――. 2002. *Democratic Phoenix: Reinventing Political Activism.* Cambridge: Cambridge University Press.

————. 2004. *Electoral Engineering: Voting Rules and Political Behavior.* Cambridge: Cambridge University Press.

O'Donnell, Guillermo. 1973. *Modernization and Bureaucratic Authoritarianism: Studies in South American Politics.* Berkeley: Institute of International Studies, University of California.

Palmer, Robert R. 1959. *The Age of the Democratic Revolution: Vol. 1. The Challenge.* Princeton, NJ: Princeton University Press.

————. 1964. *The Age of the Democratic Revolution: Vol. 2. The Struggle.* Princeton, NJ: Princeton University Press.

Pateman, Carole. 1970. *Participation and Democratic Theory.* New York: Cambridge University Press.

Paxton, Pamela. 2002. Social Capital and Democracy: An Independent Relationship. *American Sociological Review* 67: 254–77.

Peeler, John. 1998. *Building Democracy in Latin America.* Boulder, CO: Lynne Rienner.

Pinkney, Robert. 2003. *Democracy in the Third World.* 2nd ed. Boulder, CO: Lynne Rienner.

Plumb, J.H. 1967. *The Growth of Political Stability in England, 1675–1725.* London: Penguin.

Posner, Richard. 1997. Equality, Wealth and Political Stability. *Journal of Law, Economics and Organization* 13: 344–65.

Powell, G. Bingham. 1982. *Contemporary Democracies: Participation, Stability and Violence.* Cambridge, MA: Harvard University Press.

Pradhan, Menno and Martin Ravallion. 2000. Measuring Poverty Using Qualitatative Perceptions of Consumption Adequacy. *American Economic Review* 82 (3): 462–71.

Przeworski, Adam. 1986. *Capitalism and Social Democracy.* New York: Cambridge University Press.

————. 1991. *Democracy and the Market.* New York: Cambridge University Press.

————. 2004. Economic Development and Transitions to Democracy. Unpublished paper. http://ww.nyu.edu/gsas/dept/politics/faculty/przeworski/papers/TRANSWP.pdf

————. 2005. Democracy as an Equilibrium. *Public Choice* 123: 253–73.

Przeworski, Adam, Michael Alvarez, Jose Antonio Cheibub, and Fernando Limongi. 1996. What Makes Democracies Endure? *Journal of Democracy* 7 (1): 39–55.

————. 2000. *Democracy and Development: Political Institutions and Well-Being in the World, 1950–1990.* New York: Cambridge University Press.

Przeworski, Adam and Fernando Limongi. 1993. Political Regimes and Economic Growth. *Journal of Economic Perspectives* 7: 51–69.

————. 1997. Modernization: Theories and Facts. *World Politics* 49: 155–83.

Putnam, Robert D. 1993. *Making Democracy Work: Civic Traditions in Modern Italy*. Princeton, NJ: Princeton University Press.

Putnam, Robert D. 1995. Bowling Alone: America's Declining Social Capital. *Journal of Democracy* (January): 65–78.

———. (2000). *Bowling Alone: The Collapse and Revival of American Community*. New York: Simon & Schuster.

Reddy, Sanjay G. and Thomas W. Pogge. 2002. How Not to Count the Poor. http://www.socialanalysis.org.

Remmer, Karen. 1993. The Political Economy of Elections in Latin America, 1980–1991. *American Political Science Review*, 87: 393–407.

———. 1995. New Theoretical Perspectives on Democracy. *Comparative Politics* (October): 103–22.

———. 1997. Theoretical Decay and Theoretical Development: The Resurgence of Institutional Analysis. *World Politics* 50: 34–61.

Richard, Patricia Bayer. 2006, March 17. Sociopolitical Violence, Participation, and Democatic Norms in Eight Latin American Nations. Paper presented at the Latin American Studies Association, San Juan, Puerto Rico.

Robinson, William I. 1996. *Promoting Polyarchy: Globalization, U.S. Intervention, and Hegemony*. Cambridge: Cambridge University Press.

———. 2003. *Transnational Conflicts: Central America, Social Change, and Globalization*. London: Verso.

Rose, Richard, William Mishler, and Christian Haerpfer. 1998. *Democracy and Its Alternatives: Understanding Post-Communist Societies*. Baltimore: Johns Hopkins University Press.

Rose, Richard and Christian Haerpfer. 1998. *New Democracies Barometer V: A 12-Nation Survey. Studies in Public Policy No. 306*. Glasgow, Scotland: Centre for Public Policy, University of Strathclyde.

Rosenstone, Steven J. and John Mark Hansen. 1993. *Mobilization, Participation and Democracy in America*. New York: Macmillan.

Ross, Edward A. *The Principles of Sociology*. New York, 1920.

Rueschemeyer, Dietrich, Evelyne Huber Stephens, and John D. Stephens. 1992. *Capitalist Development and Democracy*. Cambridge: Cambridge University Press.

Sartori, Giovanni. (2001). How Far Can Free Government Travel? In Larry Diamond and Marc F. Plattner, eds., *The Global Divergence of Democracies*, 52–62. Baltimore: Johns Hopkins University Press.

Schumpeter, Joseph A. 1943. *Capitalism, Socialism and Democracy*. London: Allen and Unwin.

———. 1950. *Capitalism, Socialism and Democracy*, 3rd ed. New York: Harper and Row.

Schur, Lisa, Todd Shields, and Kay Schriner. 2003. Can I Make a Difference? Efficacy, Employment and Disability. *Political Psychology* 24: 119–49.

Schwartzman, Kathleen C. 1980. *Social Origins of Democratic Collapse: The First Portuguese Republic in the Global Economy.* Lawrence: University of Kansas Press.

Searle, John. 1995. *The Construction of Social Reality.* New York: Free Press.

Seers, Dudley. 1969. The Meaning of Development. *International Development Review* 11(2): 2–6.

Seligson, Mitchell A. 1978. Development and Participation in Costa Rica: The Impact of Context. In *Citizen and State: Political Participation in Latin America.* edited by John A. Booth and Mitchell A. Seligson. 145–154. New York: Holmes and Meier.

———. 2002. The Renaissance of Political Culture or the Renaissance of Ecological Fallacy. *Comparative Politics* 34: 273–92.

———. 2005. Improving the Quality of Survey Research in Democratizing Countries. *PS, Political Science & Politics:* 51–6.

Seligson, Mitchell A. and John A. Booth, eds. 1979. *Politics and the Poor: Political Participation in Latin America, Vol. 2.* 2 vols. New York: Holmes and Meier Publishers.

Seligson, Mitchell A., Annnabelle Conroy, Ricardo Cordova Macias, Orlando J. Perez, and Andrew J. Stein. 1995. Who Votes in Central America? A Comparative Analysis. In *Elections and Democracy in Central America, Revisited,* edited by Mitchell A. Seligson and John Booth. 151–182. Chapel Hill: University of North Carolina Press.

Sen, Amartya. 1976. Poverty: An Ordinal Approach to Measurement. *Econometrica* 44 (2): 219–31.

———. 1981. *Poverty and Famines: An Essay of Entitlements and Deprivation.* Oxford: Oxford University Press.

———. 1991. Welfare, Preference and Freedom. *Journal of Econometrics* 50: 15–29.

———. 1994. Freedom and Needs. *The New Republic* (January 10): 7.

———. 1999. *Development as Freedom.* New York: Random House.

Sen, Amartya and Himanshu. 2005. Poverty and Inequality in India. *Economic and Political Weekly* (September 18, pp. 4247–63 and September 25, pp. 4361–75).

Seymour, Charles. 1915. *Electoral reform in England and Wales: The Development and Operation of the Parliamentary Franchise, 1832–1885.* New Haven: Yale University Press.

Shapiro, Ian. 2003. *The State of Democratic Theory.* Princeton, NJ: Princeton University Press.

Sheth, D. L. 1999. Secularization of Caste and the Making of the New Middle Class. *Economic and Political Weekly* (August 21): 2502–10.

Shils, Edward. 1965. Charisma, Order, Status. *American Sociological Review* 30, 199–213.

Shin, Doh Chull. 1999. *Mass Politics and Culture in Democratizing Korea.* New York: Cambridge University Press.

Shivakumar, Sujai. 2003. The Place of Indigenous Institutions in Constitutional Order. *Constitutional Political Economy* 14: 3–21.

Smith, Peter H. 2005. *Democracy in Latin America: Political Change in Comparative Perspective.* New York: Oxford University Press.

Sobrevilla, Natalia. 2002. The Influence of the European 1848 Revolutions in Peru. In *The European Revolutions of 1848 and the Americas*, edited by Guy Thomson, 191–216. London: Institute of Latin American Studies.

Sorensen, Georg. 1993. *Democracy and Democratization.* Boulder, CO: Westview Press.

Sullivan, J. L. and J. E. Transue. 1999. The Psychological Underpinnings of Democracy: A Selective Review of Research on Political Tolerance, Interpersonal Trust, and Social Capital. *Annual Review of Psychology* 50: 625–50.

Teixeira, Ruy. 1992. *The Disappearing American Voter.* Washington, DC: Brookings Institution.

Testi, Arnaldo. 1998. The Construction and Deconstruction of the U.S. Electorate in the Age of Manhood Suffrage, 1830s–1920s. In *How Did They Become Voters? The History of Franchise in Modern European Representation*, edited by Raffaele Romanelli, 387–414. The Hague: Kluwer Law International.

UNDP. 2004. *Democracy in Latin America: Towards a Citizens' Democracy.* New York: United Nations Development Programme.

UNDP. 2005. *Human Development Report, 2005.* New York: United Nations Development Programme.

Vanhanen, Tatu. 1997. *Prospects for Democracy: A Study of 172 Countries.* London: Routledge.

Varshney, Ashutosh. 2000. Why Have Poor Democracies Not Eliminated Poverty? *Asian Survey* 40, 718–36.

———. 2001. "Ethnic Conflict and Civil Society: India and Beyond." *World Politics*, 53 (April), 362–398.

Verba, Sidney, Nancy Burns, and Kay Schlozman. (1997). Knowing and Caring about Politics: Gender and Political Engagement. *Journal of Politics* 59 (4): 1051–72.

Verba, Sidney and Norman H. Nie. 1972. *Participation in America: Political Democracy and Social Equality.* New York: Harper & Row.

Verba, Sidney, Norman H. Nie, and Jae-On Kim. 1971. *The Modes of Democratic Participation: A Cross-National Comparison.* Vol. 1, *Comparative Politics Series.* Beverly Hills: Sage Publications.

———. 1978. *Participation and Political Equality: A Seven-Nation Comparison.* Cambridge, MA: Cambridge University Press.

Verba, Sidney, Kay Lehman Schlozman, and Henry Brady. 1995. *Voice and Equality: Civic Voluntarism in American Politics.* Cambridge, MA: Harvard University Press.

Vilas, Carlos M. 1997. Participation, Inequality and the Whereabouts of Democracy. In *The New Politics of Inequality in Latin America*, edited by Douglas Chalmers, Carlos Vilas, Katherine Hite, Scott Martin, Kerianne Piester, and Monica Segarra, 3–42. Oxford: Oxford University Press.

Wade, Robert H. 2004. Is Globalization Reducing Poverty and Inequality? *World Development* 32 (4), 567–89.

Weiner, Myron. (1963). *Political Change in South Asia.* Calcutta: K. L. Mukhopadhyay.

Weyland, Kurt. 2005. Neoliberalism and Democracy in Latin America: A Mixed Record. *Latin American Politics and Society* 46, (1): 135–64.

White, Howard. 2002. Combining Quantitative and Qualitative Approaches in Poverty Analysis. *World Development* 30 (3): 511–22.

Winham, Gilbert R. 1970. Political Development and Lerner's Theory: Further Test of a Casual Model. *American Political Science Review* 64: 810–81.

Wolfinger, Raymond E. and Steven J. Rosenstone. 1980. *Who Votes?* New Haven, CT: Yale University Press.

World Bank. 2002. *World Development Indicators 2002.* Multiple user ed. Washington, DC: World Bank.

World Bank. 2005. *World Development Report, 2005.* Washington, DC: World Bank.

World Bank. 2006. *World Development Report, 2006.* Washington, DC: World Bank.

Yadav, Yogendra. 1999. Electoral Politics in the Time of Change: India's Third Electoral System, 1989–99. *Economic and Political Weekly* (August 21): 2393–99.

Yadav, Yogendra. 2000. Understanding the Second Democratic Upsurge: Trends of Bahujan Participation in Electoral Politics in the 1990s. In *Transforming India: Social and Political Dynamics of Democracy*, edited by Francine Frankel, Zoya Hasan, Rajeev Bhargava, and Balveer Arora, 120–145. Oxford: Oxford University Press.

You, Jong-Sung and Sanjeev Khagram. 2005. A Comparative Study of Inequality and Corruption. *American Sociological Review* 70 (1): 136–57.

Ziblatt, Daniel. 2006. How Did Europe Democratize? *World Politics* 58: 311–38.

Index